SELF-GROWTH
IN FAMILIES

Kinetic Family Drawings (K-F-D)

Research and Application

SELF-GROWTH IN FAMILIES

Kinetic Family Drawings (K-F-D)
Research and Application

By Robert C. Burns
Director, Seattle Institute of Human Development

BRUNNER/MAZEL, Publishers • New York

Library of Congress Cataloging in Publication Data

Burns, Robert C.
    Self-growth in families.

    Bibliography: p.
    Includes index.
    1. Kinetic family drawing test. I. Title.
[DNLM: 1. Child development. 2. Family.
3. Projective technics – In infancy and
childhood. 4. Art. WS 105.5.E8 B976s]
BF698.8.K53B87   618.92'89075   81-21659
ISBN 0-87630-305-X   AACR2

Copyright © 1982 by Robert C. Burns

Published by
BRUNNER/MAZEL, INC.
19 Union Square
New York, New York 10003

MANUFACTURED IN THE UNITED STATES OF AMERICA

FOREWORD

How does the child feel about himself? And especially about self in relation to family group? Psychologists have long sought an answer to this important question. The test described in the present volume quite possibly gives the clearest clues yet available.

Self-Growth in Families, third in a series, takes the reader or the practitioner a big step forward in an understanding of the possibilities of the Kinetic Family Drawing test. It is a next step in a logical but nevertheless dramatic sequence.

The first book in the series presents the thesis that in drawing every member of his family doing something, the subject reveals a great deal more about himself than in the simpler and more conventional task of drawing a family. The second volume, of substantial practical use for the individual already intrigued by this concept, provides the authors' interpretations at a symbolic level for objects commonly depicted in K-F-D drawings. It also discusses various styles of drawing as well as themes which commonly appear.

The author describes the purpose of the present book as being "to demonstrate and summarize the use of the K-F-D as a scientific tool and as a practical clinical tool in the art of therapy." He has clearly succeeded in both objectives.

His goal is for the clinician to learn to be able to read the child's drawing as one would a book. He has come a long way in making this objective possible. Reading this volume is one of the more dramatic adventures I personally have experienced in the always dynamic field of projective techniques. This book does, indeed, read like a novel.

As Piotrowsky earlier managed a computerized evaluation of the Rorschach response, Burns is now working on, and here provides projections into, a quantification of the scoring or evaluation of K-F-D variables which will permit not only demonstration of the validity and reliability of this test but also a computerized handling of data. Suggestions for future research also include the idea of a grid which superimposed over the KFD would measure the self vs. other figures as well as the distance of self from other figures, and which could define "superiority" or "inferiority" in terms of size of self or placement on the grid.

The theory behind the K-F-D test has been throughout that the child's response as seen in this test can show often much better than his own words how he feels about himself as a member of his family. The author points out that "In the process of identification the self grows by internalizing the feelings and values of the parental figures. If the parental feelings and values internalized are positive and growth producing, the child may develop a healthy, positive self-image." (Or, of course, the opposite.)

The ample illustrations in the present volume show dramatically the extent to which a child can reveal his or her feelings, not only in ordinary living but in such special circumstances as divorce, child abuse, alcoholism or other aberrations within the family. In the instance of divorce the child's drawings can, in the author's experience, sometimes help parents make and accept decisions about custody. Or, in one drawing shown, a father, an alcoholic, is pictured as so horrible by his 13-year-old son that he (the father) actually agreed to seek help from Alcoholics Anonymous.

For many children, the need for early intervention and family counseling can be defined by the K-F-D. In addition, changes in the K-F-D Self help to measure the effectiveness of counseling. The inclusion of developmental norms is gratifying and the presentation of longitudinal studies in self-development is especially intriguing. As with other projective techniques, this test shows itself as capable of reflecting changes in the individual's feelings about self and about life with the passing of time or change in actual life situation.

Another direction in which the use of this test has developed is the suggestion that adults in a family seeking professional help be asked to draw their own K-F-Ds. These, like those of their children, can often reveal more than the individual might have been able to tell in words. (It is provocative for the reader to imagine what kind of K-F-D he or she might have made as a child.)

An extremely useful and practical appendix clues readers in to the meaning of such salient items as characteristics of strokes, size and placement of drawings, meaning of different kinds of hair, facial features, body parts and other basic variables. These meanings can and should be mastered by any clinician serious about the interpretation of his patient's drawings. This test is clearly not a tool for amateurs. Special illustrations emphasize the contrast between what the casual observer sees in certain drawings and what the trained clinician sees. It gives beginners a warning not to jump at seemingly obvious conclusions as to what a drawing means.

In my estimation this is a treasure of a book about a treasure of a test. The author is to be congratulated that in the few years since the appearance of *Kinetic Family Drawings* he and colleagues have carried this amazingly revealing test so far.

Louise Bates Ames
Chief Psychologist,
Gesell Institute of Human Development

PREFACE

Kinetic Family Drawings (K-F-D) (1970) was an attempt to share the excitement of a projective technique which had been clinically helpful to the author. Actions, Styles and Symbols in Kinetic Family Drawings (1972) was a more detailed discussion of the K-F-D with some attempt to stimulate research as well as clinical use.

By continuing work with families directly or in consultation, my own knowledge of K-F-D has grown. In teaching courses in recent years in developmental psychology, projective techniques, and art therapy, the use of the words "self" and "self-portrait" in the literature appears over-inclusive. According to the literature, self-portraits may be obtained from all psychological projective techniques as well as a host of other "personality" tests. According to Buck, drawing a house reveals a self-portrait, drawing a person yields a self-portrait, and drawing a tree gives a self-portrait. Handwriting analysis is said to reflect a self-portrait; body language yields a self-portrait, etc. The term "self-portrait" has come to mean most anything and everything revealing about a person. Thus the term "self-portrait" is too vague to mean anything in a repeatable, scientific framework.

Many years ago, after listening to my bewildering classroom discussion of a myriad of self-portraits revealed by psychological techniques, a medical student startled me by saying, "If you ask Picasso to draw a picture of a person or a tree, he may draw a picture of any person or any tree. If you ask Picasso to draw a self-portrait, you may actually get a self-portrait of how Picasso views Picasso."

So Kinetic-Family-Drawing was born. I started to gather self-portraits within a kinetic family matrix. How persons see themselves within a family may be different from how they see themselves outside the family.

The K-F-D reliability and validity studies have proved revealing, as have works such as that by O'Brien and Patton (60) in preparing the K-F-D for computer analysis.

It has been gratifying these past ten years to have worked with many students on their K-F-D theses and dissertations. Of equal satisfaction have been the cross-cultural contacts made in Argentina, Brazil, Canada, Great Britain, Germany, Holland, Italy, Japan, Poland, Norway, and South Africa, where K-F-Ds are gathered fairly extensively. I would particularly like to thank Takamasa Kato of Japan, M. Souza de Joode of Brazil, and Gunther Huber of Germany (all listed in references), for communications and exchange of K-F-Ds, helping me to understand Japanese, Brazilian, and German families. I would appreciate expanding this cross-cultural exchange and hope others so inclined would share with me.

My special thanks to my son, Carter Burns, for his energy, patience and skill in helping to prepare the manuscript.

This book represents an effort to share the results of ten more years of K-F-D use and research. The art and the science of understanding self-growth in the nuclear family and substitute families through K-F-D analysis are joyfully continued.

Robert C. Burns

CONTENTS

Foreword by Louise Bates Ames   v

Preface   ix

1. INTRODUCTION   3
   Drawings 1-6

2. THE NUCLEAR SELF AND THE ENVIRONMENTAL
   SELF   17
   Figures 1, 2
       I. Comparison of D-A-P, H-T-P, D-A-F,
          and K-F-D   20
       Drawings 7-40

3. K-F-D RESEARCH FINDINGS   62
       I. Some Historical Studies in Children's Art   62
      II. Analysis of Human Figure Drawing as Psychological
          Tests   62
          A. Draw-A-Person Test (D-A-P)   62
          B. House-Tree-Person (H-T-P)   63
          C. Draw-A-Family Test (D-A-F)   63
          D. Kinetic Family Drawing (K-F-D)   63
     III. Other Psychological Tests Related to K-F-D   63
      IV. Cross-cultural K-F-D Research Findings   64
       V. K-F-D Developmental Norms   65

   VI. K-F-D Reliability Studies   65

  VII. K-F-D Validity Studies   66
       Table 1: Inter-scorer Reliability Summary
       Chart   66

4. K-F-D RESEARCH MANUAL 68
    I. Procedure for Obtaining K-F-Ds   68
   II. Example of K-F-D Computerized Study   69
     A. General Self-concept   70
     B. Social Self and Peers   70
     C. School and Academic Self-concept   70
     D. Aggression   70
     E. Hostile Isolation   71
  III. Directions for Quantifying K-F-D Actions   71
       Table 2: K-F-D Raw Drawing Variables for
       Descriptive Statistics   72
       Table 3: Definition of K-F-D Action Raw
       Drawing Variables   73
       Table 4: Definition of K-F-D Figure
       Characteristics Raw Drawing Variables   74
       Table 5: Definition of K-F-D Positional, Distance,
       and Barrier Characteristics Raw Drawing
       Variables   75
       Table 6: Scoring Criteria for Figure Activity
       Level   75
       Table 7: Scoring Criteria for Figure
       Ascendence   76
       Table 8: Scoring Criteria for Figure
       Communication Level   76
       Table 9: Scoring Criteria for Figure
       Cooperation   76
       Table 10: Scoring Criteria for Figure
       Direction   77
       Table 11: Scoring Criteria for Masochism   77
       Table 12: Scoring Criteria for Figure
       Narcissism   77
       Table 13: Scoring Criteria for Figure
       Nurturing   78
       Table 14: Scoring Criteria for Figure
       Sadism   78
       Table 15: Scoring Criteria for Figure
       Tension   78
       Table 16: Scoring Criteria for Body   79

Table 17: Scoring Criteria for Roots (size of feet)   79

Table 18: Scoring Criteria for Size of Figures (millimeters)   79

Table 19: Scoring Criteria for Arm Length   80

Table 20: Scoring Criteria for Eyes   80

Table 21: Scoring Criteria for Facial Expression   80

Table 22: Scoring Criteria for Face   81

Table 23: Scoring Criteria for Parent Missing   81

Table 24: Scoring Criteria for Number of Sibs Present   81

Table 25: Scoring Criteria for Teeth Present   81

Table 26: Scoring Criteria for Number of Barriers   82

Table 27: Orientation Between Figures   82

Table 28: Scoring Criteria for Styles   82

Table 29: Scoring Criteria for Like-to-Live-In-Family (LILIF)   82

IV. Clinical and Computer Interpretations of a K-F-D   83

Drawing 41

A. Artistic Analysis of K-F-D 42   84

Drawing 42

B. Computer Analysis of K-F-D 42   84

Table 30: Raw Computer Variables for K-F-D 42   86

V. Instructions for Judging Kinetic Family Drawings (K-F-Ds) and Styles   87

A. Style – Compartmentalization (COMPART)   88

B. Style – Edging   89

C. Style – Encapsulation (ENCAPS)   90

D. Style – Folding Compartmentalization (FOLCOM)   91

E. Style – Lining on the Bottom (LINBOT)   92

F. Style – Lining at the Top (LINTOP)   93

G. Style – Underlining Individual Figures (UNDLIF)   94

H. Style – Bird's Eye View (BIRDIV)   95

VI. K-F-D Grid   96

VII. Ways of Viewing K-F-Ds   96
       Figures 3, 4

5. IDENTIFICATION WITHIN THE FAMILY
   FOR BETTER OR FOR WORSE.................   99
       I. Parental Identification Leading to Positive
           Self-image   100
          Drawings 43-48
      II. Parental Identification Leading to Negative Self-
           image   112
          Drawings 49-53

6. INABILITY TO IDENTIFY WITHIN THE NUCLEAR
   FAMILY   121
       I. The Separated Child   121
          A. Divorce   121
          B. Which Parent Should the Separated Child Live
              With?   122
             Drawings 54-59
          C. Which Culture Should the Separated Child Live
              In?   130
             Drawings 60, 61
             Foster and Adoptive Home Placement   134
             Group Home Versus Foster Home   134
             Drawings 62, 63
             Foster Home or Own Home   138
             Drawings 64, 65
             The Rejecting Parent   142
             Drawing 66
             The Tuning-out Parent   144
             Drawings 67, 68
             Workaholic Parent   148
             Drawings 69, 70
             Alcoholic Parent   152
             Drawing 71
             Battering Parent   154
             Drawing 72
             Psychotic Parent   156
             Drawing 73
             Homosexual Parent   158
             Drawing 74
             Missing Parent Idealized   160
             Drawing 75

Identification with Objects Rather than
  People   162
Drawings 76, 77
Runaways   164
Drawing 78

7. LACK OF SELF-GROWTH:
   THE DEPRESSED AND SUICIDAL CHILD 166
       I. No Faces   166
          Drawings 79-81
      II. Seeking Excitement and Warmth   169
          Drawings 82, 82A, 83
     III. Moon Children: Depression and Suicide   174
          Drawings 84-90
      IV. Parental Rejection – Suicide   186
          Drawings 91, 92

8. LONGITUDINAL STUDIES IN SELF-DEVELOPMENT . 189
       I. Daniel from Ages 3 to 11: A Struggle for
          Identity   189
          Drawings 93-102
      II. Bill from Ages 3 to 11: The Outsider   206
          Drawings 103-107
     III. Diane from Ages 5 to 7: Withdrawal   214
          Drawings 108-112

9. K-F-D USE IN SELF-GROWTH:
   CHILD ABUSE, FOSTER AND ADOPTIVE HOME
   PLACEMENT, FAMILY THERAPY 223
       I. K-F-D Use in Child Abuse   223
          Drawing 113
      II. Counseling and Foster Home Placement for
          Sally   226
          Drawings 114-116
     III. Evaluation of Therapy: Scott, a Case of Severe
          Anxiety Reaction   231
          Drawings 117-119
      IV. Evaluation and Counseling: The Case of
          David   234
          Drawings 120-122
       V. Family Therapy: K-F-D in Color – The Three
          Sisters   238
          A. Sister #1: Sally, Age 8 – The Baby   238
             Drawing 123

  B. Sister #2: Jill, Age 13 – The Outgoing,
     Competitive Sister   240
     Drawing 124
  C. Sister #3: Cathy, Age 17 – The Introverted,
     Competitive Sister   242
     Drawing 125
  VI. Family Therapy: Dependence – Parent and Child
      K-F-Ds   244
      Drawings 126-128
  VII. Dependency on an Alcoholic Father   250
       Drawing 129

10. K-F-D AND OTHER PROJECTIVE TESTS 252
    Drawings 130, 131

11. CONCLUSION 254

    Appendix 256

    References 269

    Index 273

SELF-GROWTH
IN FAMILIES

Kinetic Family Drawings (K-F-D)

Research and Application

CHAPTER 1

INTRODUCTION

The Kinetic-Family-Drawing (K-F-D) provides one tool for measuring family dynamics, including the development of the self within various family matrices. By family we mean a husband, wife, and one or more children. We can, in addition, speak of the extended family which may include grandparents, relatives, etc., or the substitute family such as that in group, foster, or communal living.

Our first K-F-D book (13) is an introduction to the use of the K-F-D in understanding the drawer in the family. Our second K-F-D book (14) provides an interpretive manual for K-F-D actions, styles, and symbols. This book focuses on application and research with K-F-Ds, along with some new dimensions of K-F-D interpretation (15, 16).

K-F-Ds have a special language telling us a great deal about family interactions, if we speak the language. Most of us are visually illiterate, however, and miss the valuable, rich, documented sources of personal and interpersonal information that are caught and fixed in K-F-Ds.

To a great extent, what is experienced and seen in a K-F-D is determined by the interpreter's history, interests, preoccupations, and expectations. A Nigerian friend of mine chuckled thoughout a perusal of the 1972 K-F-D book. He particularly enjoyed the relationship between the animals in the K-F-Ds and the human figures and saw the animals in a way that I had missed. Thus, a doctor may see illness; a banker, money; a vain person, styles; a sexy person, sex; an angry person, anger; a humorous person, humor.

The following questions are offered to demonstrate the wide range of possible experiences while analyzing a K-F-D:

What is your first impression? Who and what do you see? What is happening? How do you feel about what is happening?

What do you notice about physical intimacy or distance? Is the K-F-D warm or cold, soft or hard, pleasant or unpleasant?

Are people touching or are they shut off from each other? Who is facing whom?

How do people in the K-F-Ds feel about their bodies? Are they using their bodies to show off? To hide? To be seductive? Are they proud of their bodies? Ashamed?

Who's ascendent? Who's descendent?

Are the K-F-D "people" happy, sad, sadistic, suffering, blank, bored, rigid, strong, involved, detached, angry, subservient, trusting, or satisfied?

How does the group relate? Are they tense or relaxed? What are their messages towards each other? Do you feel love present?

Is it a family you would like to be a member of?

Perhaps all of us interested in human drawing analysis should learn to draw people. It is difficult to imagine a person capable of drawing only stick-like, blank-faced people being able to "see" deeply into drawing analyses. For such look-but-don't-see people I would recommend study of *The Zen of Seeing* (29) or *Drawing On the Right Side of the Brain* (28) as helpful in overcoming drawing visual illiteracy. Our goal is to learn to read K-F-Ds as you would read a book, from left to right (or right to left), then vertically. Go over the K-F-D again and again, each time trying to pick up something you have missed.

We may receive a K-F-D as a list of static objects, i.e., tables, chairs, people, arms, feet. With practice and increasing understanding we may focus on the kinetic-family-drawing-self (K-F-D-S).

What if the K-F-D could "come to life"? What would be happening? Who would go, who would stay? Who would succor? Who would nurture? Who would love, who would hate? What energies, if any, are flowing from father? Mother? Self? What are the barriers to the energy flow?

In an excellent K-F-D validating study, O'Brien and Patton (60) did a statistical analysis of many K-F-D variables through computer programming, relating these K-F-D variables to external criteria. As part of their summary, O'Brien and Patton say, "The two most important variables in predicting a child's social self-concept are the orientation of the father toward the self figure (ORDS) and the direction of the father figure in relation to all the other figures in the drawing (FACEDA). The children who drew the father figure facing the self figure had a greater

DRAWING 1

Dad
Drinking

Mom

Self
(13)

Brother (16)
Reading

social and peer self concept than those children who drew the father facing in another direction."

If the orientation of the father toward the self figure (ORDS) is critical to social self-concept, what has happened to the self-concept of the drawer of K-F-D 1? If the drawing "came to life," what would happen? Would you like to be a member of this family? Are the energies flowing from the father positive or negative? Who in the family is looking at the drunk-crazed father? Who would dare? What has happened to the cocooned self? Where are family members' feet? What do the buttons on the father symbolize? Does this 13-year-old boy "identify" with the father and want unconsciously to be his dad? Is this a "healthy" family for a self to grow?

Twelve-year-old Michael lived with his father and a younger brother Rick in the city. The parents are divorced. One other brother lived in a foster home and one lived with the mother. The father was mostly Irish-American; the mother was a full-blooded native American. The sons occasionally visited the mother who had returned to the reservation. When asked to make a K-F-D of his city family, Michael produced Drawing 2.

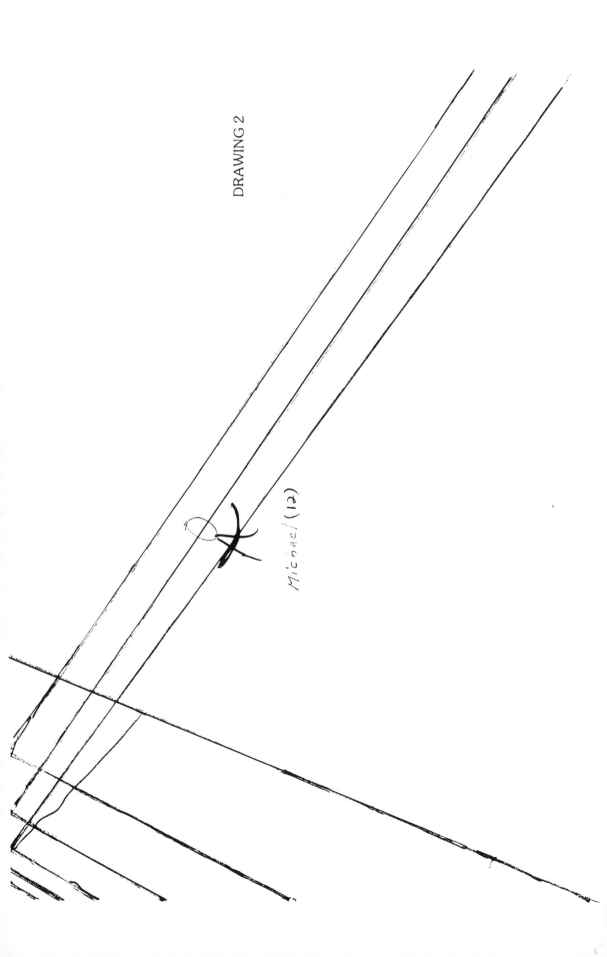

DRAWING 2

Michael (12)

When on the same day Michael was asked to make a K-F-D of his family on the reservation he did Drawing 3.

In which family setting does Michael have a chance for self-growth? Is this guess a clinical "hunch" or can we quantify the difference in the K-F-Ds so that a judge could use the results as part of his decision to place Michael in a growing environment? Both parents want Michael to live with them. Could we convince the father through Michael's K-F-D to allow Michael to live with the mother? (There will be more about Michael later in our book.) Can the K-F-D be one method used to insure optimal placement in divorce, foster, and adoptive home placement? Can we measure self-growth in a family?

DRAWING 3

Consider the development of Jack as reflected in his K-F-Ds. Our second book (14) ended with a description of Jack, age 11. Let us review and continue with Jack's K-F-D story. Jack had been living with his mother and stepfather. The mother had been hospitalized on four occasions with severe bouts of mental illness. She had a history of erratic behavior, including frequent beatings of Jack. She had met the present stepfather in a mental institution and he had a history of paranoia. He was extremely threatening and occasionally violent toward Jack. At age 11, while Jack was living with the mother and stepfather, he produced Drawing 4.

Note the tiny size of Jack and his encapsulation. He is faceless and helpless-appearing. His feet are missing; the absence of feet is suggestive of feelings of instability, but in Jack's case the omission has added significance. When feet are firmly "planted on the ground," they suggest that the self has roots. Jack's lack of feet suggests a lack of roots in this family matrix.

DRAWING 4

Jack had begged to live with the true father and this was finally arranged. Three months after moving into his new home, Jack produced Drawing 5.

In this family, Jack has developed a face. The increase in size of the K-F-D Self (K-F-D-S) is striking. The barriers between family members have been removed. However, we see in Jack's features and position an identification with brother, Andy, age 1½. At this stage, Jack acted in a very immature way (soiling, babytalk, etc.).

DRAWING 5

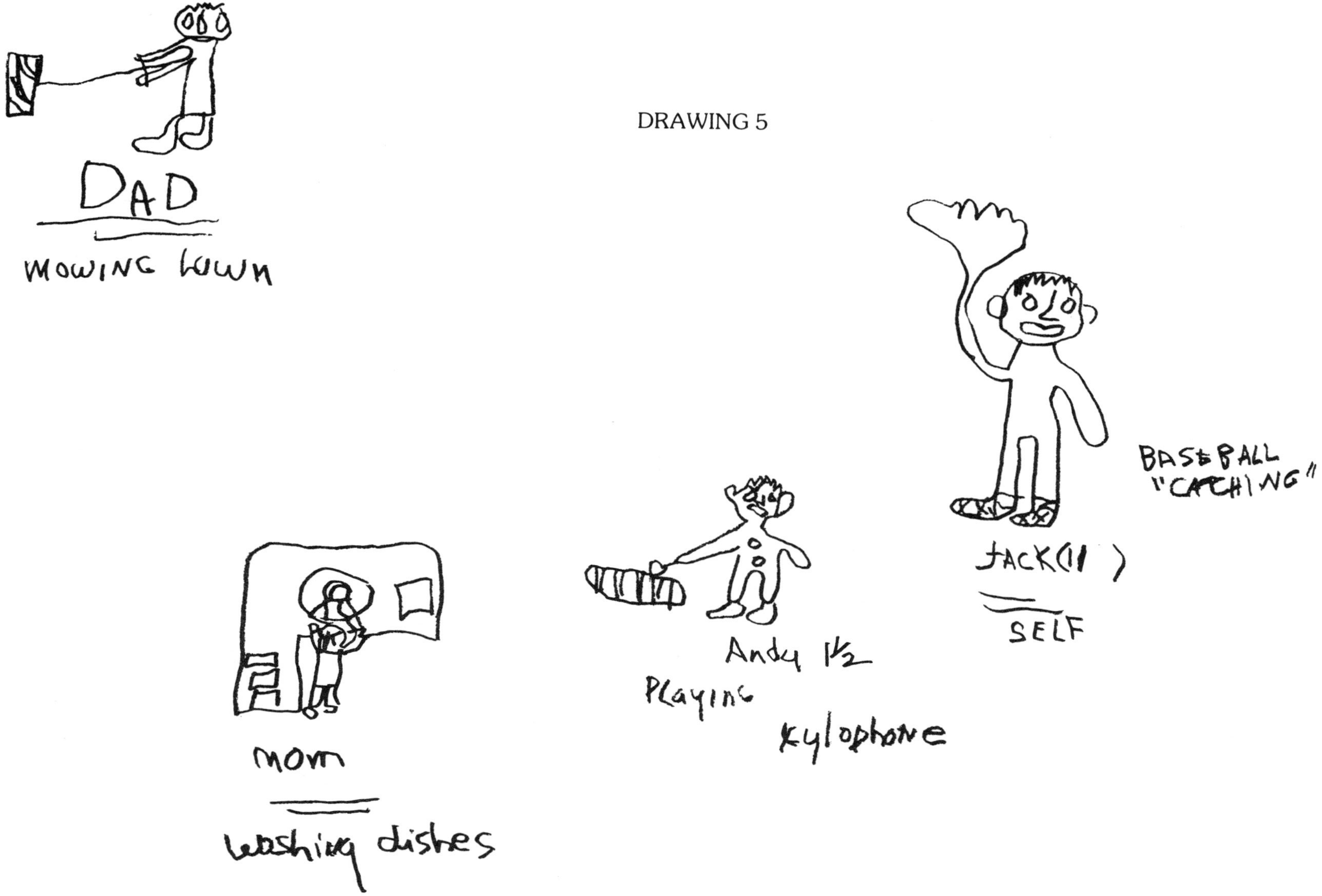

DAD
MOWING lawn

Andy 1½
Playing
xylophone

BASEBALL
"CATCHING"

JACK (1)
SELF

mom
washing dishes

DRAWING 6

Mom
COOKING

Dad
"Edging"

self mowing

Baby
Playing with blocks

Nine months later, in this same family, Jack, now 12, produced Drawing 6. Jack has lost his baby appearance; the "baby" is now smaller than Jack and at the bottom of the page in a subordinate position. In facial appearance, body, and position, Jack looks like the father and identifies with him. Jack has progressed from a tiny, faceless, encapsulated, helpless K-F-D-S to a grimly determined K-F-D-S with face, freedom to grow, and identification with father.

Jack has a long way to go in this family matrix. The faceless mother and the rather grim, cutting father suggest Jack may "roll on" as suggested by his lack of feet.

However, Drawing 6 suggests an ongoing process of identification between father and son. Jack has a more realistic approach to life without barriers between himself and the parents. He is striding toward goals, depicted by the moving profile K-F-D-S, in contrast to the full-faced stationary K-F-D-Ss shown in Drawings 4 and 5. Jack has completed one phase of development in the atmosphere of his true father's home, including identification with his father. This process has given Jack improved self-confidence, self-control, self-direction, and a self capable of loving and being loved by people and, thus, potential to grow. Jack's self-growth as measured from his K-F-D-S is as shown.

Jack at age 11 living
with his mother

Jack at age 12 living
with father

This growth in Jack's self-image is clear and measurable. Living in a family matrix with the true father has produced more growth than had occurred in 11 years with the real mother. This growth has been clinically validated against school achievement, behavioral improvement, and more adequate social adjustment.

Draw-A-Person Jack: Age 12

But does the drawing of the self in the K-F-D (K-F-D-S) produce any different data than if the drawer is asked to Draw-A-Person (D-A-P)? The D-A-P has been said by Machover to "represent the expression of self, or the body, *in the environment*" (54). Just what is the difference in the K-F-D-S and the D-A-P? Is one the "inner person" and one the "outer person"? Is one the child, the other the adult? Is Jack in the home a very different personality from the personality evidenced outside the home?

The comparison of the K-F-D-S and the D-A-P as related to self-development is the subject matter of our next chapter.

CHAPTER 2

THE NUCLEAR SELF AND THE ENVIRONMENTAL SELF

From the Gods comes the saying: "Know thyself"
— Juvenal

This above all: to thine own self be true.
— William Shakespeare

The word "personality" comes from the word persona or mask as used in ancient Greek plays to depict symbolic others. A person may wear many "masks" or have many outer "layers" of personality. One suspects the inner layer, when all masks are stripped away, reflects the self as shaped in the early years of family life. Perhaps the K-F-D-S reflects this inner self and techniques such as the D-A-P depict a layer of "personality" covering up the more basic self-image.

Kurt Lewin's (52) well-known formula is $B = f(P, E)$; all behavior is a function of the nature of the person and of his environment. Machover (54), one of the pioneers in D-A-P analysis, spoke of the D-A-P as representing "an expression of the self in the environment," i.e., *the environmental self*. Perhaps the K-F-D self represents an expression of the self as formed in early family life, i.e., *the nuclear self*.

In transactional analysis terms, perhaps the K-F-D-S more closely portrays the child and the Draw-A-Person Self (D-A-P-S) portrays the adult. We know, for example, if we score the mental age of the K-F-D-S as compared to the mental age of the D-A-P-S, the K-F-D-S will score significantly younger. We know the figure obtained by the

D-A-P technique is similar to the "person" obtained by the House-Tree-Person technique in that each technique calls for the drawing of a person on a single sheet of paper. Buck says, "Each of the drama wholes (House, Tree, Person) is to be regarded as a *self-portrait* as well as the drawing of a specific object" (10).

When I used to lecture medical students about psychological techniques and told them a tree or a house or a person was a self-portrait, they often stared unbelieving. In 12 years as chief psychologist in a children's hospital, I attended morning, noon, and night conferences (endocrinology, neurology, radiology, etc.) at which *slides, charts,* or *x-rays* of some sort were presented to the physician audience and viewed with interest. It slowly dawned on me that at psychology conferences, where words were presented, the physician became restless and drowsy, and those who remained till the end were skeptical. Some would scoff and say, "I don't *see* what you are talking about," or "Let's see the Self." So, for my skeptical physician friends I made *slides* and *pictures* of the Self.

Following are two lectures I prepared for residents and interns so they would stay awake for my psychology conferences.

LECTURE NUMBER ONE
A STYLUS AND A PENCIL

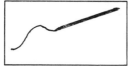

This is a stylus. It is attached to the brain by wires and electrodes and records brain waves.

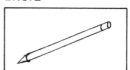

This is a pencil. It is attached to the brain by bones, flesh and nerves.

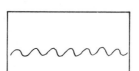

This is a brain wave recorded from the brain. It is normal.

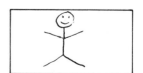

This is a Self recorded from the brain. It is normal.

This is an abnormal brain wave.

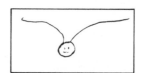

This is an abnormal Self.

Figure 1 — The stylus and the pencil are both scientific recording instruments attached to the brain.

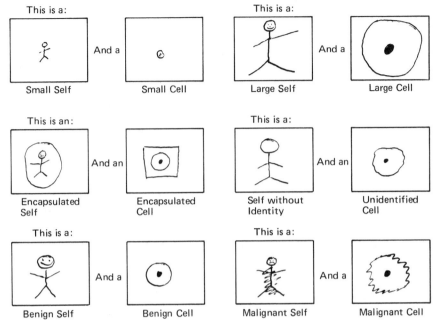

Figure 2 — The Cell and the Self

Following my "Cell and Self" lectures, the skeptics would say, "We know that is a cell, but how do we know that is a Self?

I explained that I had the patient draw-a-person (D-A-P), an old psychological test by Goodenough (34) and the "person" reflected a self-image. If that didn't work, I further explained, I would give a House-Tree-Person test and get three more self-portraits.

As mentioned in the Preface, a friendly but skeptical medical resident suggested that if I wanted a self-portrait, why not be direct and ask for one? So the Kinetic-Family-Drawing technique began in which a self-portrait was drawn in a kinetic family matrix.

After gathering some K-F-Ds and comparing them to the D-A-Ps it was evident the resident was correct; the "person" obtained in the D-A-P was usually unlike the "self" obtained in the K-F-D.

19

I. COMPARISON OF D-A-P, H-T-P, D-A-F, AND K-F-D

Consider four drawings by 11-year-old George, all obtained on the same day. George's D-A-P is shown in Drawing 7.

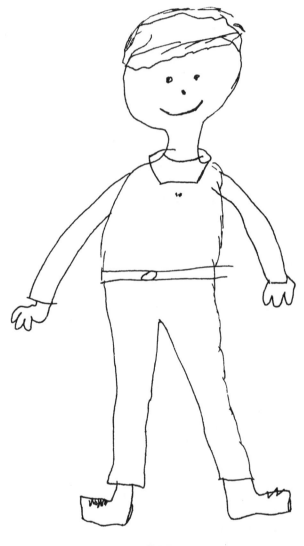

DRAWING 7

The drawing has no outstanding distortions and seems essentially normal. George's H-T-P shows a figure with buttons, suggesting dependency, and rather a small head, as shown in Drawing 8.

DRAWING 8

Drawing 9 was obtained from George using the instructions for Draw-A-Family (D-A-F). The D-A-F Self seems to be a composite of the figures from George's D-A-P and H-T-P. Ears are present, and the drawing shows no significant distortions. When George was asked to make a K-F-D, he produced Drawing 10.

SELF (11)   BROTHER (13)   MOM   DAD

DRAWING 9

The K-F-D-S is very different from those obtained in the other drawings. There is no face and the Self is precariously balanced on a ladder. The other figures are faceless and in compartments. The K-F-D-S reflected the extreme tension in the home. Outside the home, George was well-behaved, as reflected in the D-A-P-S. Inside the family, the extreme tension associated with numerous problems is reflected in the incomplete and tense-appearing K-F-D-S.

22

DRAWING 10

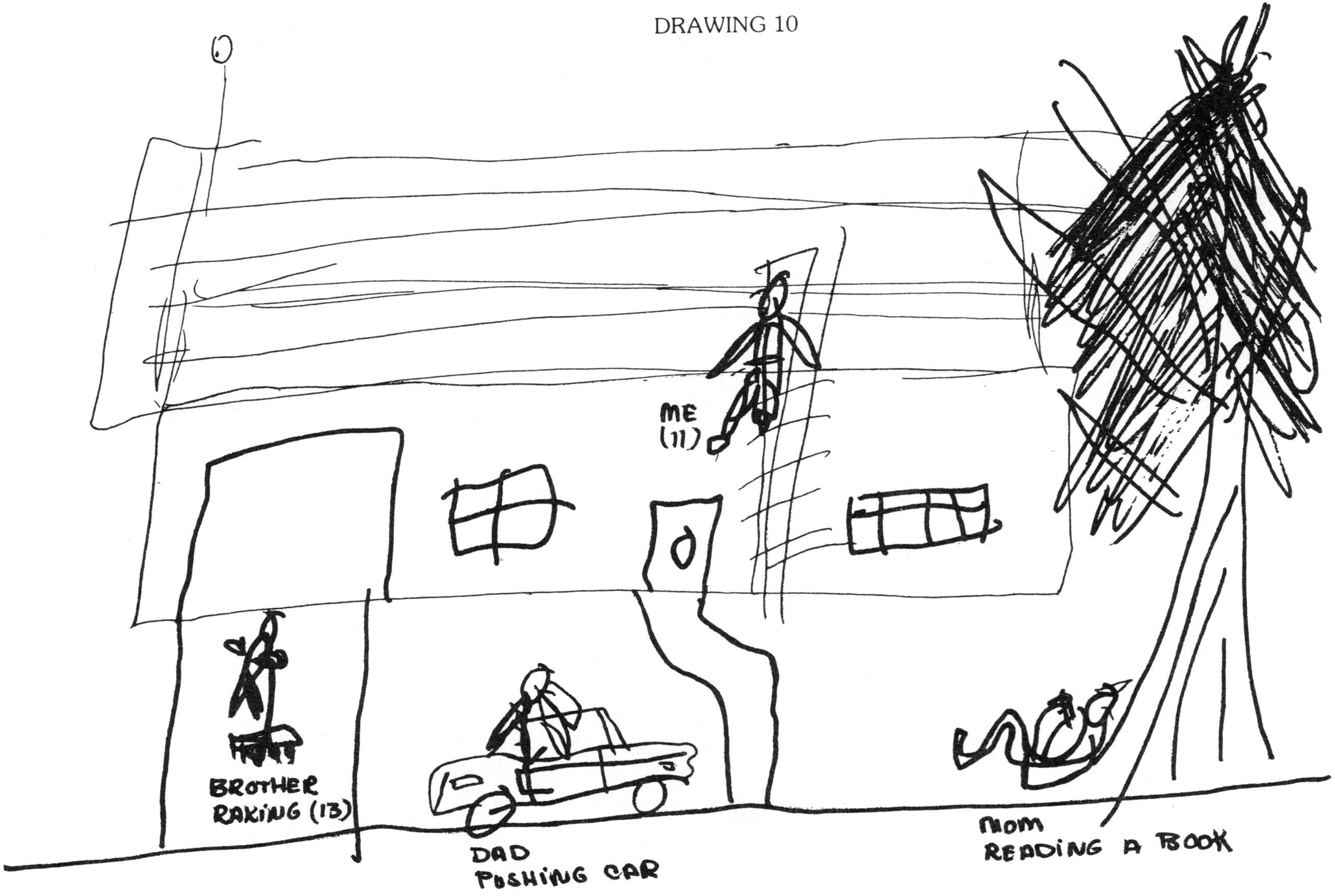

MOM
READING A BOOK

ME
(11)

DAD
PUSHING CAR

BROTHER
RAKING (13)

Bright 5¾-year-old Jill produced the next series of drawings. To the D-A-P instructions, Jill produced Drawing 11 and included her dog. Jill's D-A-P seems normal.

DRAWING 11

Jill's H-T-P drawing is shown in Drawing 12. The H-T-P figure is similar to that obtained in the D-A-P, except the arms are missing.

DRAWING 12

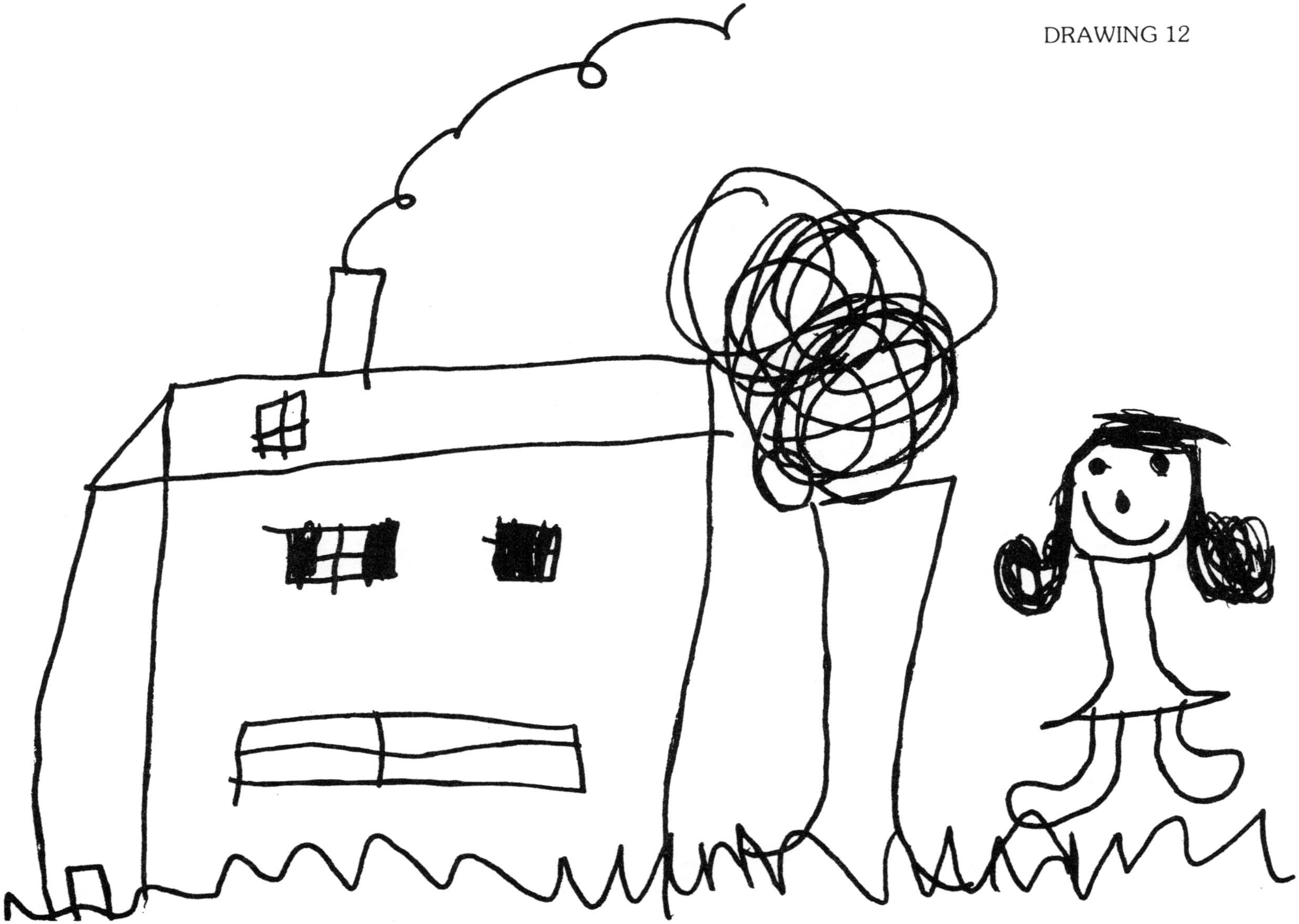

In Drawing 13, we see Jill's response to the D-A-F test. The D-A-F Self is quite similar to those obtained in the D-A-P and H-T-P pictures.

On the same day that the other three tests were given, Jill was asked to produce a K-F-D. Her K-F-D is shown in Drawing 14. The K-F-D-S is strikingly different from the Selves obtained in Jill's other drawings. The 3-year-old brother had recently been seriously ill and had been home from the hospital only a few days. Jill's K-F-D-S is "keeping an eye on him" and is hypervigilant and "tied up" by her tensions concerning her brother's well-being.

This delightful, bright, little girl was quite normal *outside* the family, as reflected by the D-A-P and D-A-F tests. *Inside* the family, she was a bundle of nerves and reacted as one might expect from her K-F-D-S.

DRAWING 14

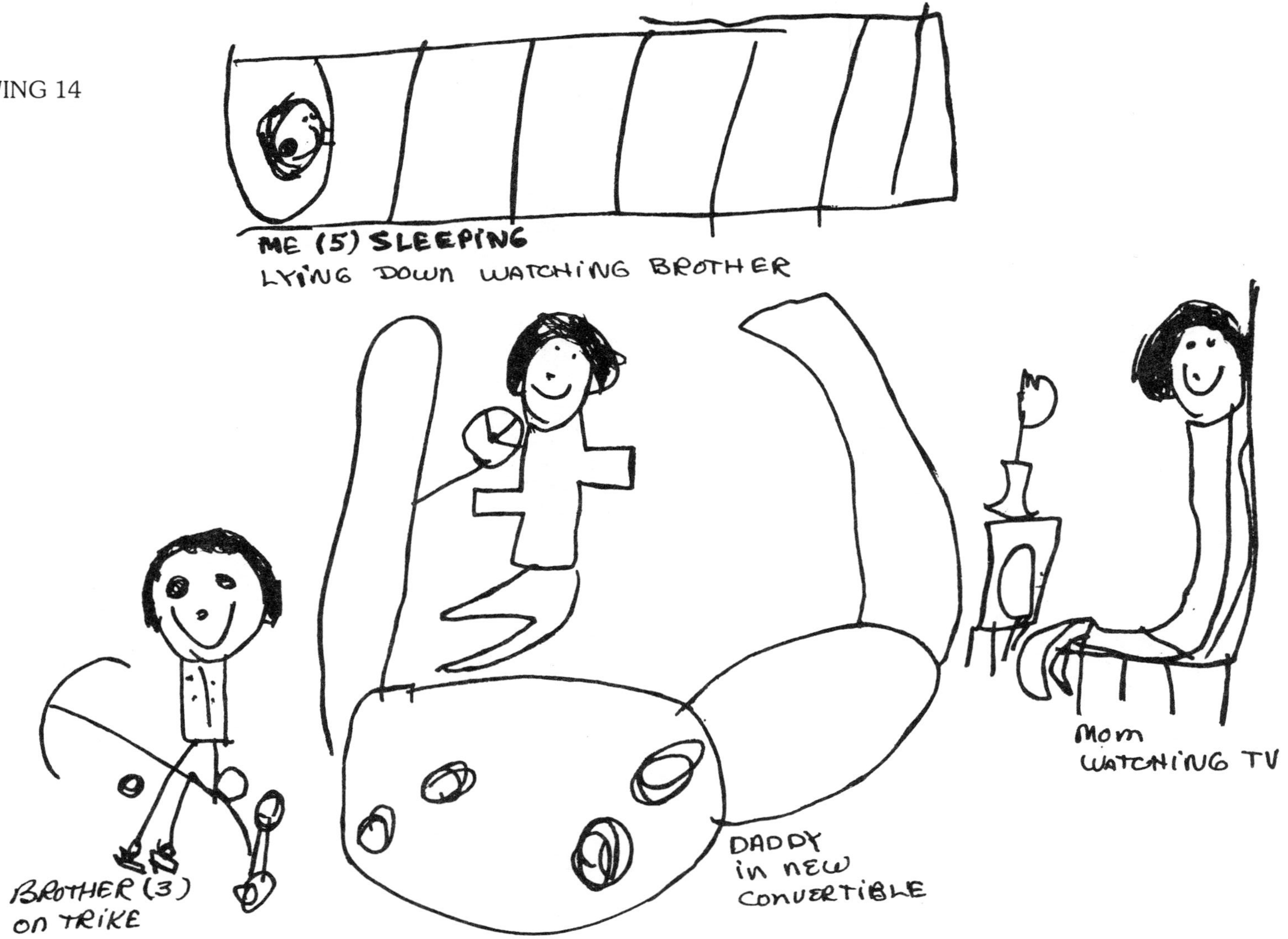

ME (5) SLEEPING
LYING DOWN WATCHING BROTHER

MOM
WATCHING TV

DADDY
IN NEW
CONVERTIBLE

BROTHER (3)
ON TRIKE

Let us examine in greater detail the relation of the D-A-P and the K-F-D-S. D-A-P and K-F-Ds in this section were obtained in the same session with use of standard instructions.

DRAWING 15

Six-year-old Julie's D-A-P is shown in Drawing 15. Her K-F-D is shown in Drawing 16. Here, dad is picking up his hat and her identification with him is suggested by the positions of dad and the K-F-D-S. The mother is smaller, in a subordinate position in the family, and eating. Julie has long hair like mother and sister and, thus, is feminine in the drawing. Yet, her D-A-P seems to reflect her desire to be like or with dad, although in reality she is feminine and "big sister" in the family. The D-A-P figure is dad and reflects Julie's identification with him as one of her "selves." Her K-F-D reflects Julie's self within the nuclear family.

DRAWING 16

teresa (2)
Hanging up
clothes

Brian (5)
Putting away
blocks

Brett (9)
Playing ball

Julie (7)
washing dishes

Dish

Dad
picking up
hat

Mother - eating hamburger

Drawing 17, a D-A-P by 12-year-old Mary, appears to be that of a football player. Mary's K-F-D is shown in Drawing 18. In her K-F-D, the football player turns out to look like Mary's 6-year-old brother. The brother has an incomplete face, as does Mary. Brother is being "mean."

Mary has long hair like the girls in the K-F-D (except "Mommy"). Her D-A-P appears to be a wish or an obsession to be like an aggressive young brother. In the family matrix, she is passive and demanding and acts like a 6-year-old. Outside the family, she is something of a tomboy, as in the D-A-P.

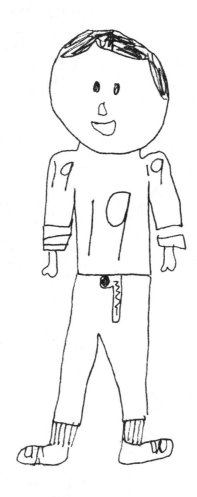

DRAWING 17

DRAWING 18

Someone threw ball
thru window – She caught it

Hitting Someone

Mary
Playing cards
with Friend

Me (12)
throwing ball

David
6

Billy

Mommy

saying "ow"

eating

Karen

Daddy
sore ear

bowl

Mark
"crying"

Ted, age 10¾, made Drawing 19, his D-A-P, which shows an Afro hairstyle and buttons.

DRAWING 19

In Ted's K-F-D, Drawing 20, we see a K-F-D-S very similar to that in his D-A-P. There is a consistency in the self-image and Ted seems to be the "same" person both in and out of the family.

DRAWING 20

mom
lying down

brother standing
16

sister
13

DAD

sister
15

4

brother sitting

8
9
7

3

ball

brother
daydreaming
3

2

sister
6

sister
8

6

me (1034)

5

The D-A-P of 16-year-old Tim is seen in Drawing 21. Tim's D-A-P appears to be that of a superman with no neck and no feet, a very independent (no neck) figure.

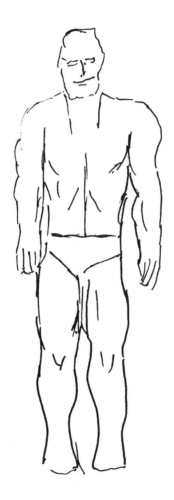

DRAWING 21

Drawing 22 shows Tim's K-F-D. He refused to put himself in the family. Tim's K-F-D father and mother are separated and engrossed in their own worlds. Tim's dad, an "executive," turns his back on his wife and is absorbed in his work. Tim wants no place in this family and appears to be growing like "self-sufficient" dad.

Ham Radio

Dad working

Cat + Mom

DRAWING 22

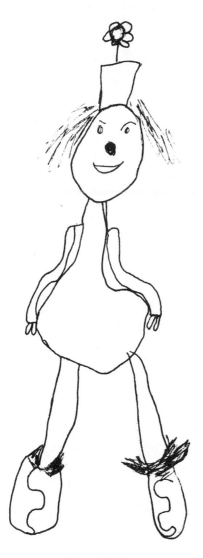

DRAWING 23

Drawing 23, by 9½-year-old Dick, is that of a clown.

Dick's K-F-D is shown in Drawing 24. His K-F-D-S is tiny and immature compared to his D-A-P. The dad is yelling to the mother for food. In Dick's family, the father acted like a child and competed with the children for mother's attention. He continually belittled Dick. Outside the family, Dick acted the role of the clown. He covered his feelings of inferiority by making people laugh with him rather than at him. Inside the family, Dick could not control the belittling and felt helpless. He acted in a very immature and demanding fashion. Outside the family, Dick acted out the D-A-P; inside the family, he acted out the K-F-D-S.

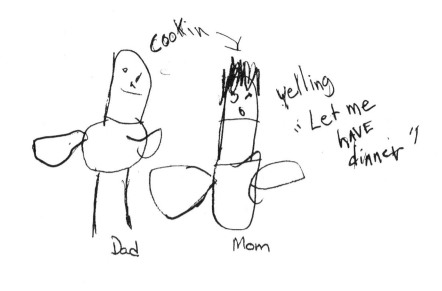

Cookin →

yelling "Let me HAVE dinner"

Dad   Mom

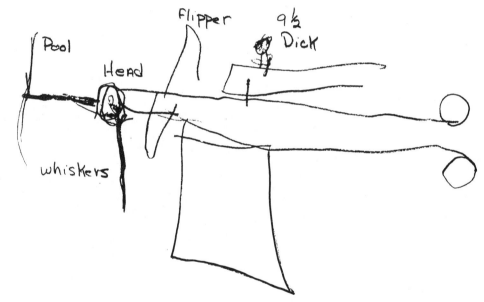

Pool

Flipper

9½ Dick

Head

whiskers

DRAWING 24

a "ghost"

Debby "Snoopy" trick or treat

Ed, age 16½, made Drawing 25. He declined to complete a whole figure.

DRAWING 25

Drawing 26 is Ed's K-F-D. He refused to include himself in the picture but placed himself on the other side – a tiny, bare-faced figure "driving in the country" (Drawing 26A).

The D-A-P face is that of the mustachioed older brother, who was just graduated from high school. In his fantasy, Ed identified with the strength and power of the strong older brother. In actuality, Ed was the unhappy, relatively ineffectual person portrayed in the K-F-D-S.

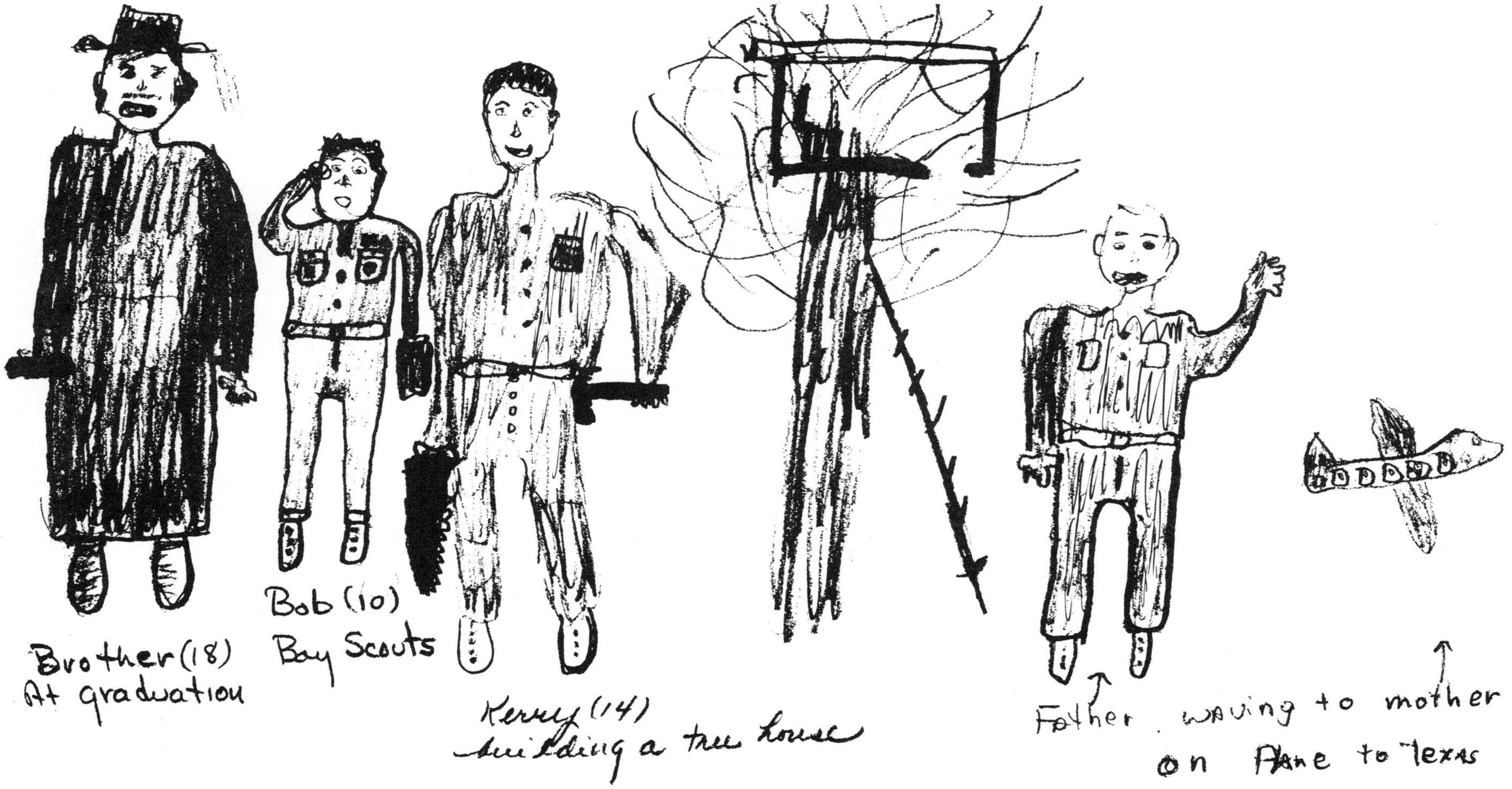

Brother (18)
At graduation

Bob (10)
Boy Scouts

Kerry (14)
building a tree house

Father, waving to mother
on Plane to Texas

DRAWING 26

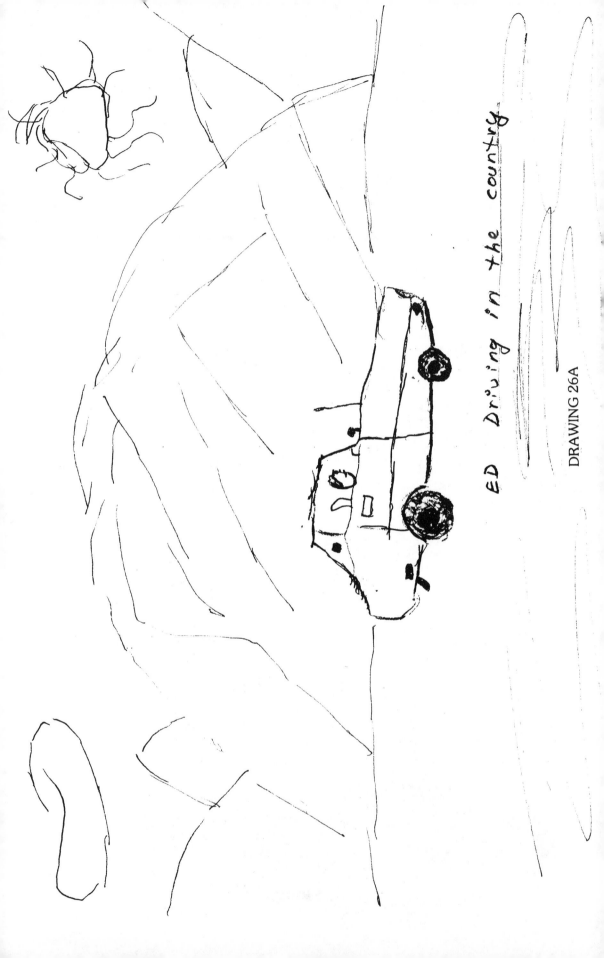

ED Driving in the country

DRAWING 26A

DRAWING 27

Martha, age 9, produced Drawing 27. The D-A-P seems to be a boy with buttons. Martha's K-F-D is seen in Drawing 28. The 8-year-old brother looks like the D-A-P. This brother is the father's favorite. Note how the K-F-D-S is closely hovered near the mother. The father is "not home." the D-A-P figure seems to reflect Martha's partial identification with her brother as a way to be loved by the missing dad. In the real family, her needs are met by the mother, and Martha's K-F-D-S is vigilant and demanding of mother's attention.

DRAWING 28

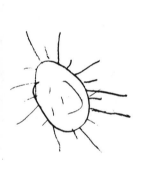

Dad not home

Cleaning the room

Emma jo
sisters
15
Jackie (3)

little
dolly

me (9)
watching
them

Mom
handing them
the widner

Andy tony Patty
(4) going to store

louie-brother (8)
Cleaning the yard

Drawing 29 was made by 13½-year-old Greg. His D-A-P is that of a vacant-eyed, "tough guy," although one arm is missing.

DRAWING 29

Greg's K-F-D is shown in Drawing 30. At the time the K-F-D was made, Greg was living in his 13th foster home. Note the baby-like appearance of the K-F-D-S close to the cooking mother. Outside the family, Greg was described as a bully. Inside the family, he was described as demanding, whiny, and jealous of anyone interrupting his "mothering." Greg has developed a passive-aggressive personality. If his dependency needs are met, he acts like the K-F-D-S. If they are unmet, he becomes aggressive like the D-A-P.

DAVID (16) PLAYING FOOTBALL

ME (13½) SINGING

MOM COOKING

BROTHER (11) EATING

DAD DRIVING

DRAWING 30

Sally, age 10½, produced Drawing 31. Note the shading of the body and, particularly, the *overemphasized eyes.*

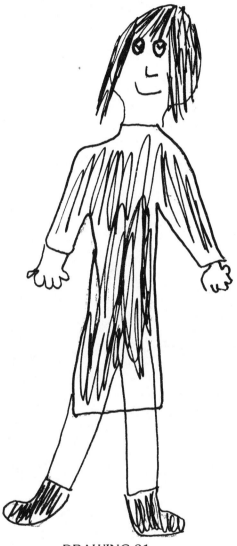

DRAWING 31

Drawing 32 is Sally's K-F-D. Everyone in the family is "hiding" except the 5-year-old. All the figures are heavily shaded – even the sun is blackened. The mother's eyes are exaggerated, much more so than the K-F-D-S. Sally's D-A-P eyes may partially reflect Sally's identification with her mother's suspicious nature. Mother had a diagnosis of paranoia.

DRAWING 32

DRAWING 33

In Drawing 33, by 14-year-old Dan, we note the eyes and the shaded, bound-up feeling.

Dan's K-F-D is shown in Drawings 34 and the other side, 34A. In the K-F-D, Don drew his father first, then the legless mother. He turned the paper over and drew the K-F-D-S, brother, and younger sister. Note the sister's eyes are the only ones similar to those in the D-A-P. At the time of the drawing, Dan had a fetish for women's and girls' shoes. He would steal them and keep them in his room. The father was a very athletic man, who lifted weights and "kept himself in shape." Don had a severe reading disability but excelled in sports. At times, he acted like his father and wished to be like him. At other times, he wanted to be younger than his sister. The D-A-P seems to be a combination of the father's strength and the sister's eyes and seems to combine Don's wish at times to be one or the other. The K-F-D-S was more his actual Self in the family setting – a boy who was obsessed with achieving in sports.

51

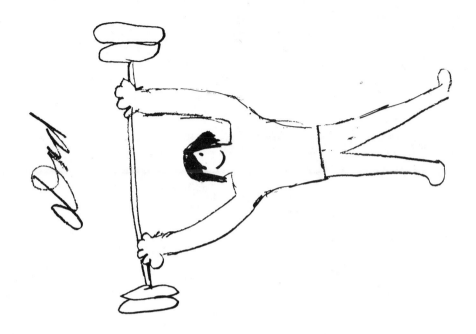

DRAWING 34

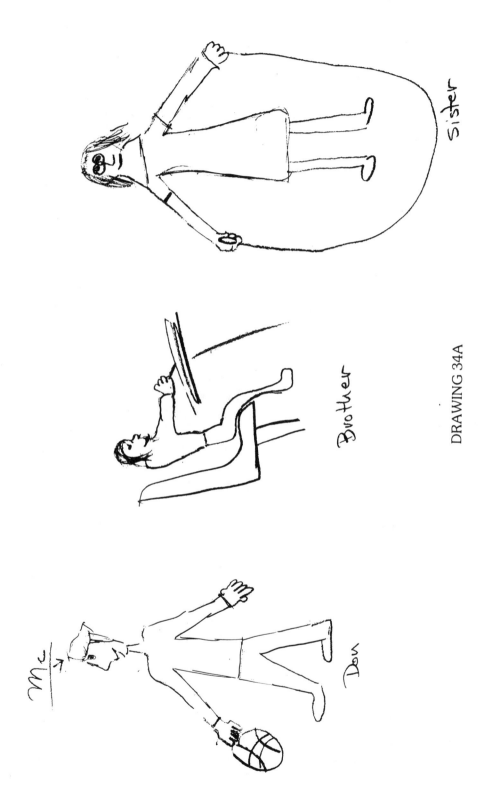

Sister

Brother

Me

Don

DRAWING 34A

Drawing 35 is by rebellious 13-year-old Becky – that of a witch.

Becky's K-F-D is shown in Drawing 36. Becky refused to put her parents in the picture. She referred to her mother as a witch. Her D-A-P suggested her obsessive desire to rid herself of the witch. The K-F-D-S shows the teenage rebel out of the family and in the park, which was where Becky often went to meet her friends and get away from the "witch."

DRAWING 35

DRAWING 36

At The Park
Me (13)

Linda 18

Sister Smoking

Bill 16

Tom 15

Marie 5

Holding a baby Kitty

Refuses to Put in Parents

Drawing 37, by 10-year-old Todd, shows a hitchhiker "moving out."

DRAWING 37

Todd's K-F-D is shown in Drawing 38. The K-F-D-S is very immature and Todd is in his compartment. His domineering older brother is "above" him. Todd comes from a very high-achieving family. He has a great deal of pressure to be successful. The D-A-P reflects Todd's wishes to get away from responsibility. In the family, he is immature but identifies with his dad (and his wishes). He tries to please him and become a doctor "like dad and grandad." The D-A-P suggests, however, that it will be a real struggle for Todd to assume a responsible role and fight the urge to "hit the road."

DRAWING 38

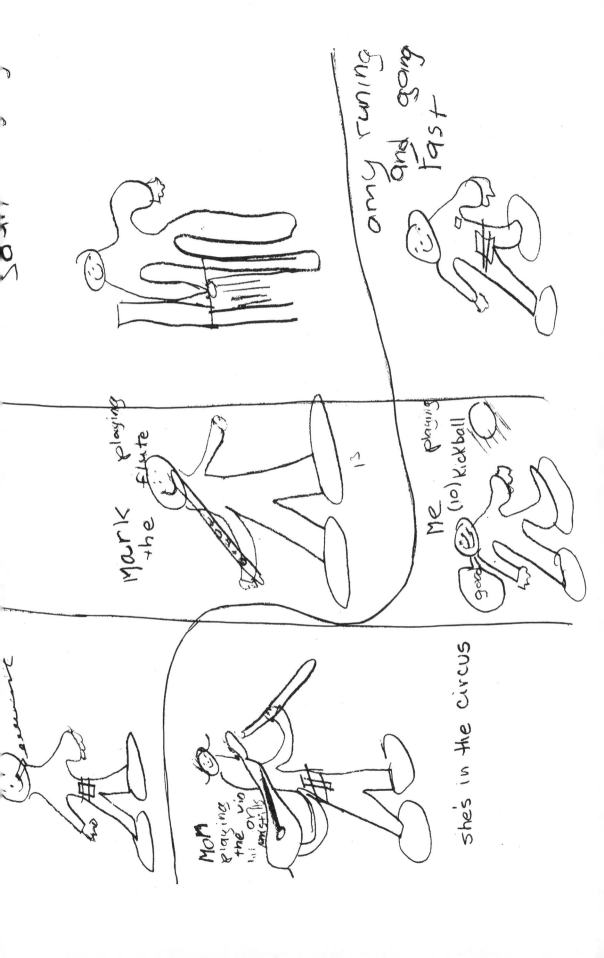

Drawing 39, a D-A-P by 13-year-old Adam, suggests a tormented, angry face and an incomplete person.

DRAWING 39

As can be seen in Adam's K-F-D, Drawing 40, there is no K-F-D-S, only an "X." The style used in this drawing is folded compartmentalization, which is associated with acute emotional disturbance. Adam refused to be part of this family and the intense torment and anger seen in the D-A-P face reflect his anger and disturbance associated with his lack of family identification.

DRAWING 40

ad

Mom

dy

feeding
rabbits

listening to my
stereo

16

e

Mona

X

ren

Dave

Handball

CHAPTER 3

K-F-D RESEARCH
FINDINGS

I. SOME HISTORICAL STUDIES IN CHILDREN'S ART

Bender (5) and Despert (25) have pioneered in the psychological interpretation of the art of disturbed children. Anatasi and Foley (2) made an early exhaustive survey of the literature concerning artistic behavior in the abnormal and of spontaneous drawings by children in different cultures. Alschuler and Hattwich (1) contributed to the appreciation of children's painting. Raven (62) described an imaginative technique in which the child was asked to draw and, while drawing, to imagine and describe a series of events.

More recently DiLeo (26) has discussed children's art with emphasis on development and deviant characteristics and on the use of drawings as diagnostic aids. The comprehensive work of Koppitz (46) has focused on a systematic evaluation of multiple aspects of human figure drawings of children age five to twelve. Dennis (24) has studied group values through children's drawings. Schildkraut et al. (65) have studied human figure drawings in adolescence.

II. ANALYSIS OF HUMAN FIGURE DRAWING AS PSYCHOLOGICAL TESTS

A. Draw-A-Person Test (D-A-P)

In 1926 Florence Goodenough published *Measurement of Intelligence by Drawing* (33). A child was told to "Draw a Person," and the drawings were scored for mental age. The Goodenough D-A-P Test soon became an accepted and widely used psychological test of intelligence. In 1963, D.B. Harris revised the D-A-P and established separate norms for boys and girls (36).

B. House-Tree-Person Test (H-T-P)

Buck (10) introduced the House-Tree-Person (H-T-P) test in 1948. A child was asked to draw a house, a tree, and a person. Clinical interpretations of the drawings were made. The H-T-P was one of the first uses of human figure drawings for psychological projective tests. Catalogs such as that of Jolles (41) described in great detail the symbolic interpretations of the house, the tree, and the person.

C. Draw-A-Family Test (D-A-F)

The earliest reports found in the literature on family drawings are those by Hulse (38) who described a Draw-A-Family Test. Aside from studies by Reznikoff and Reznikoff (63) and Shearn and Russell (68), no other reports of the D-A-F could be found in the literature. Hammer (35), Koppitz (46), and DiLeo (26) discuss the use of D-A-F.

D. Kinetic Family Drawing (K-F-D)

Burns and Kaufman (13,14) described a method of simply asking children to draw the members of their families including themselves doing something. It was found that the addition of action to the drawings produced more meaningful and revealing data related to the self within the family matrix.

III. OTHER PSYCHOLOGICAL TESTS RELATED TO K-F-D

In Burns and Kaufman's second book (14) the actions, styles, and symbols within the K-F-Ds were discussed. The actions, styles, and symbols in other psychological tests related to visual family interactions are closely allied to the K-F-D concepts (12).

In 1941 Buhler and Kelley introduced the World Test (11). The materials and applications are reminiscent of Doll Play studies.

The "Little World" set adopted by Bolgar and Fischer (6) consisted of 232 pieces including houses, trees, people, fences, autos, and animals. In an application, the subjects are asked to do with them whatever they like. A complete record of behavior and verbalizations is kept.

In 1947, Shneidman (69) introduced his Make-A-Picture-Story test (MAPS). In taking the test the subject constructs his own pictures from a set of 67 separate cardboard figures, any of which may be superimposed on any of 22 backgrounds presented one at a time by the examiner. This technique combined features of the World Test, Thematic Apperception Test (TAT) and psychodrama (59).

Kuthe (47, 48, 49) published three articles on social schema in which he explored the way people organize social stimuli. He used a felt-covered board upon which subjects (100 male undergraduates) were asked to place "cut-outs" of men, women, children, animals, and objects. The situation was unstructured. Kuthe found:

> a) a predominant tendency to place human figures together without interposing nonhuman objects;
> b) specific social schema showing a tendency to place a child nearer to a woman than to a man and the tendency to place a dog nearer to a man;
> c) the more positively the child feels about his parents and siblings the closer he will place these figures.

Kuthe concluded: "When people are allowed to place sets of objects cut from felt on a field, their responses are organized. There is a very strong social schema – people belong together. Human figures were grouped together to a greater degree than were nonhuman figures."

Weinstein (75), using Kuthe's Felt-Figure Technique, designed a study to test her hypothesis that emotionally disturbed children differed from normal children in the manner in which they organized social stimuli. Her results indicated that emotionally disturbed children departed from the typical schemata in that they tended to separate or isolate human figures (especially woman/child) in the experiment. The normal child would usually group the figures together, forming a close unit.

Britain (7,8) has reported that interfigure distance increases on the Family Drawing Test (FDT) following a period of stress and interpersonal anxiety.

These studies are related in having a common visual method of viewing the child as depicted in various social and family settings and may thus be correlated with K-F-D findings.

IV. CROSS-CULTURAL K-F-D RESEARCH FINDINGS

A number of studies and reports have suggested the usefulness and applicability of the K-F-D to many cultures. Kato et al. (42,43,44) have reported on its use in Japan. Freeman (31) describes its use with British children. Souza de Joode (72) demonstrated its clinical usefulness with Brazilian children. Landmark (50) mentions its use in Norway. Roth and Huber (64) have worked with the K-F-D in Germany. Burns and Kaufman's book has an edition in Great Britain (19), a Spanish (17) and a Japanese (18) edition. There is general agreement that the K-F-D styles are found in all these cultures and the technique is clinically useful and promising.

V. K-F-D DEVELOPMENTAL NORMS

MacNaughton (56) reports normative data with 314 K-F-Ds by 4- and 5-year-olds. Fifty-one percent were 4 years old; 55% were boys. In general these children were found to be both able and willing to draw K-F-Ds. Four-year-old girls elevated their mothers twice as often as 5-year-old girls, while 5-year-old boys elevated their mothers twice as often as did 4-year-old boys.

In her dissertation, Jacobson (39) reports on the developmental norms for public school children ages 6 through 9.

Thompson's (73) dissertation involved the K-F-Ds of 197 suburban adolescents ages 13 through 18: "the clearest trend is among females. Thirteen and 14-year-old females draw themselves largest most of the time; at 17 and 18, the father is drawn as the largest figure most of the time. In terms of actions older sisters are depicted as the most often involved. Males are depicted in destructive actions more often than females. Constructive actions predominate in depictions of mothers. As males get older they tend to draw more expansively. Males who draw constricted drawings at age 16 and older appear to show more social disturbance than those who are more expansive at those ages. Females, by contrast, show a greater degree of expansiveness at all ages."

Kato (42) reports a normative study on K-F-D styles carried out on 767 normal Japanese children (male:396, female:371) ages between 6 and 12. This study also records the frequency and type of emotional exchanges between family members.

VI. K-F-D RELIABILITY STUDIES

The most recent Annual Review of Psychology dealing with projective tests (3) says, "a reliable objective scoring method for Kinetic Family Drawings has been developed" (p. 560).

Many K-F-D variables allow for obvious and high reliability between raters. For example, the family size, number of sibs, size of figures, distance of figures, number of barriers, direction of figures, actions of figures, activity level of figures, and many others may be reliably measured.

McPhee (57) has done intensive work in training judges to reliably score K-F-D styles. His Reliability Summary Chart is seen in Table 1.

Table 1 offers a concise summary of the interjudge reliability data. The Pearson product-moment correlation coefficients are averages derived from Fisher's transformations used to condense the correlation matrices produced by five raters with 3 tests of 79 K-F-Ds. Table 1 reveals considerable overall agreement among the raters as to the occurrence of K-F-D styles.

O'Brien and Patton (60) used a multiple analysis of variance (MANOVA) to evaluate the possible effect of age and sex on numerous K-F-D variables. The results indicated no significant sex or age effect.

VII. K-F-D VALIDITY STUDIES

Sims (70) has reported a study of the relationship between the K-F-D and the Family Relations Indicator. Levenberg (51) has reported a study of K-F-D as related to professional training and psychodiagnostic skill. Johnston (40) has demonstrated K-F-D differences in children from intact versus divorced homes. Sobel and Sobel (71) discriminated adolescent male delinquents through the use of K-F-D. Heineman (37) demonstrated the validity of a K-F-D style (compartmentalization) in the K-F-Ds of siblings of severely emotionally disturbed children. Schornstein (66,67) reports the use of K-F-D in discrimination of child abuse. Brown (9) has used the K-F-D to discriminate effective foster home placement. McPhee (57) has shown

TABLE 1

Inter-scorer Reliability Summary Chart

Style	Pilot Study	Set 1	Set 2	Set 3
Compartmentalized	.921	.843	.867	.873
Lining on Bottom	.883	.936	.760	.890
Underlining Individual Figures	.616	.550	.675	.725
Lining at Top	.755	.853	.775	.883
Edging	.840	1.000	1.000	1.000
Folded Compartments	1.000	1.000	1.000	1.000
Total Style	.846	.880	.825	.845

the relationship between K-F-D styles and disturbed childhood behavior.

McGregor has recently completed his doctoral dissertation on the "Kinetic Family Drawing Text: A Validity Study" (55), and Lowery et al. (53) have given an overview of K-F-D research.

The studies in this chapter suggest the research possibilities of the K-F-D in contributing to the understanding of the family dynamics and factors related to self-growth within the family.

CHAPTER 4

K-F-D RESEARCH
MANUAL

This chapter defines some ways K-F-D variables may be more easily quantified for research including computerized approaches.

For K-F-D research, the following standardized approaches and scoring procedures are suggested.

I. PROCEDURE FOR OBTAINING K-F-Ds

Some K-F-D studies are difficult to interpret because the instructions varied or different size paper was used. The standard instructions appear in the second K-F-D book (14):

> The drawings are obtained individually. The subject is asked to seat himself on a chair at table of appropriate height. A sheet of plain white 8½ X 11 inch paper is placed on the table directly in front of him. A No. 2 pencil is placed in the center of the paper and he/she is asked to *Draw a picture of everyone in your family, including you, DOING something. Try to draw a whole people, not cartoons, or stick people. Remember, make everyone DOING something – some kind of action* (p. 5).

The examiner then leaves the room and checks back periodically. The situation is terminated when the subject indicates verbally or by gesture that he/she is finished. No time limit is given. Noncompliance is extremely rare. If the subject says, "I can't," he/she is encouraged periodically and left in the room until he/she completes the K-F-D."

Standard instructions and standard size paper are critical in comparing research results.

II. EXAMPLE OF K-F-D COMPUTERIZED STUDY

In recent years, researchers have started to use computers to score K-F-Ds and establish criteria for interpretation of K-F-D variables. A computerized approach was used by O'Brien and Patton (60) in their revealing K-F-D study. The subjects were 104 children from two different schools located in middle class neighborhoods. Each subject completed a K-F-D. In addition, a questionnaire composed of the Coopersmith Self-Esteem Inventory (SEI) (21) and the Children's Manifest Anxiety Scale (CMAS) (20) was administered to each child. The SEI was scored for (a) general concept; (b) social and peer self-concept; and (c) school and academic self-concept. The CMAS was scored for anxiety level.

Teachers completed the School Behavior Checklist (SBCL) (58) on each child. This checklist was scored for (a) aggressive behavior; (b) passive-aggressive behavior; (c) withdrawal behavior; (d) hostile-isolationary behavior; (e) prosocial behavior; and (f) learning-disabled behavior. All questionnaires, drawings, and SBCLs were numerically coded in order to protect the anonymity of the subjects and to allow the experimenter to correctly match the questionnaire, K-F-D, and SBCL for each subject.

Statistical analysis was performed on an IBM/370 computer, utilizing program materials supplied by BMD Biomedical Computer Programs (27) and MANOVA (23). The following procedures were performed: (a) descriptive statistics; (b) stepwise regression analysis; and(c) multiple analysis of variance.

Twenty-nine raw measures were collected from each drawing, such as family size (FAMSIZ), size of the self figure (SIZSEL), and distance from self to father (DISTSD). (See Tables 3, 4, 5, pp. 73-75.)

The raw drawing variables were subsequently combined to form 15 new variables: (a) power variables which deal with the relative size between figures, and (b) cohesion variables which involve barriers or distance. Descriptive statistics including means and standard deviations were computed for the drawing and the combined variables.

Stepwise regression was utilized to develop the predictive equations while CMAS, SEI, and SBCL variables served as the dependent variables. F level for inclusions was .01. F level for deletion was .005. The most efficient predictive equation was presented for each dependent variable.

The most important variable for predicting manifest anxiety was the activity level of the father figure (ACTDAD). The more action and strength the child attributes to the father figure, the more anxiety is present. The most efficient equation was: 1.39 (ACTDAD) + 4.67(FACESE) + 1.05(AGE) + 1.77(ACTSEL) − 1.15(ACTMON) − 5.84(ORDS) − 1.12(SIZSIB) = 3.42(FACEMO) = 1.41(SIZDAD) − 2.39(ORTOTM) − 14.54. This equation yields an $R^2 = .44$ with F = 4.31 $(p^5.01)$.

This procedure allowed O'Brien and Patton to measure several aspects of the K-F-D and then use these measures to predict three independently measured and clinically useful variables: anxiety level, self-esteem, and classroom behavior. The following is a summary of some of their findings, all of which have an F = $(p<.01)$

A. *General Self-concept*

The two most important variables for the prediction of general self-concept were the activity level of the father figure (ACTDAD) and the direction in which the self figure is facing (FACESE): the greater the activity attributed to the father figure, the less the general self-concept score; the more the self figure faces away from the other figures or into the drawing, the greater the general self-concept.

B. *Social Self and Peers*

The two most important variables in predicting the child's social self-concept are the orientation of the father toward the self figure (ORDS) and the direction of the father figure in relation to all the other figures in the drawing (DIRDAD). The children who drew the father figure facing the self figure had a greater social and peer self-concept than those children who drew the father facing in another direction.

C. *School and Academic Self-concept*

The most important variable in the prediction of the child's school and academic self-concept was the number of figures in the drawing (FAMSIZ): the larger the family, the greater the school and academic self-concept.

D. *Aggression*

The two most important variables in predicting aggressive behavior were the number of siblings (NOSIBS) and the relative size of the child and sibling figures compared with the size of the parental figures (POWKID): the greater the number of siblings in the drawing, the less

70

aggressive behavior was seen; the more aggressive child also drew himself and his siblings relatively larger in relation to his parents.

E. Hostile Isolation

The two most important variables in the prediction of hostile, isolated behavior were grade level (GRADE) and sex (SEX) of the child: the higher the grade level, the less hostile isolated behavior was seen. Also, the females tended to show more hostile isolated behavior than the males.

The work of O'Brien and Patton and others demonstrates the research of possibilities of the K-F-D in understanding family dynamics including the growth of the self in the family matrix.

III. DIRECTIONS FOR QUANTIFYING K-F-D ACTIONS

The most frequent K-F-D actions as quantified in the second K-F-D book (14) and subsequent research are listed as raw drawing variables in Table 2. Tables 3, 4, and 5 give a definition of K-F-D variables used in descriptive statistics.

The scoring criteria for descriptive statistics are given in Tables 6 through 29.

TABLE 2
K-F-D Raw Drawing Variables for Descriptive Statistics

ACTIONS			FIGURE CHARACTERISTICS			POSITION, DISTANCE AND BARRIERS			STYLES			LIKE TO LIVE IN FAMILY (LILIF)	
Variables	X	SD	Variables	X	SD	Variables	X	SD	Variables	X	SD	X	SD
ACTDAD			ARMDAD			ASCDAD			COMPART				
ACTMOM			ARMMOM			ASCMOM			EDGING				
ACTSEL			AMRSEL			ASCSEL			ENCAPS				
COMDAD			BODDAD			BARRMD			FOLCOM				
COMMOM			BODMOM			BARRSD			LINBOT				
COMSEL			BODSEL			BARRSM			LINTOP				
COOPDA			EYEDAD			DIRDAD			UNDLIF				
COOPMO			EYEMOM			DIRMOM			BIRDIV				
COOPSE			EYESEL			DIRSEL							
MASDAD			FACDAD			DISTMD							
MASMOM			FACMOM			DISTSD							
MASSEL			FACSEL			DISTSM							
NARDAD			FACEXD			ORDM							
NARMOM			FACEXM			ORDS							
NARSEL			FACEXS			ORMD							
NURDAD			FEEDAD			ORMS							
NURMOM			FEEMOM			ORSM							
NURSEL			FEESEL			ORSD							
SADDAD			NOSIBS										
SADMOM													
SADSEL			PARMSM										
TENDAD			PARMSD										
TENMOM			PARMSB										
TENSEL			SEX										
			SIZDAD										
			SIZMOM										
			SIZSEL										
			TEEDAD										
			TEEMOM										
			TEESEL										

TABLE 3
Definition of K-F-D Action Raw Drawing Variables

ACTIONS:

ACTDAD-activity level of the father
ACTMOM-activity level of the mother
ACTSEL-activity level of the self
COMMOM-communicating mother
COMDAD-communicating dad
COMSEL-communicating self
COOPMO-cooperative mom
COOPDA-cooperative dad
COOPSE-cooperative self
MASMOM-masochistic mother
MASDAD-masochistic father
MASSEL-masochistic self
NARMOM-narcissistic mother
NARDAD-narcissistic father
NARSEL-narcissistic self
NURDAD-nurturing father
NURMOM-nurturing mother
NURSEL-nurturing self
SADDAD-sadistic father
SADMOM-sadistic mother
SADSEL-sadistic self
TENDAD-tense father
TENMOM-tense mother
TENSEL-tense self

TABLE 4
Definition of K-F-D Figure Characteristics Raw Drawing Variables

Physical Characteristics:

ARMDAD-arm length of father
ARMMOM-arm length of mother
ARMSEL-arm length of self
BODDAD-body completion of father
NODMOM-body completion of mother
NODSEL-body completion of self
EYEDAD-eye of father
EYEMOM-eye of mother
EYESEL-eye of self
FACEDA-face completion of father
FACEMO-face completion of mother
FACESE-face completion of self
FACEXD-facial expression of father
FACEXM-facial expression of mother
FACEXS-facial expression of self
FAMSIZ-total number of family members in KFD
FEEDAD-size of father's feet
FEEMOM-size of mother's feet
FEESEL-size of self's feet
NOSIBS-number of siblings found in KFD
PARMSM-parent missing; mom
PARMSD-parent missing; dad
PARMSB-parents missing; both
SEX-   male or female
SIZDAD-size of the father figure (in m.m.)
SIZMOM-size of the mother figure
SIZSEL-size of the self
TEEDAD-teeth in father figure
TEEMOM-teeth in mother figure
TEESEL-teeth in self figure

TABLE 5
Definition of K-F-D Positional, Distance,
and Barrier Characteristics Raw Drawing Variables

ASCDAD-ascendent father
ASCMOM-ascendent mother
ASCSEL-ascendent self
BARRMD-number of barriers between mother and father
BARRSD-number of barriers between self and father
BARRSM-number of barriers between self and mother
DIRDAD-direction faced by father
DIRMOM-direction faced by mother
DIRSEL-direction faced by self
DISTMD-distance from mother to father
DISTSD-distance from self to father
DISTSM-distance from self to mother
DISTSS-total distance between all sibs
ORDM- orientation between father and mother
ORDS- orientation between father and self
ORMD- orientation between mother and father
ORMS- orientation between mother and self
ORSM- orientation between self and mother
ORSD- orientation between self and father

TABLE 6
Scoring Criteria for
Figure Activity Level

Activity	ACTSEL	ACTMOM	ACTDAD
Laying	0	0	0
Sitting	1	1	1
Standing	2	2	2
Reading	3	3	3
Riding	4	4	4
Doing	5	5	5
Running	6	6	6
Throwing	7	7	7
Hitting	8	8	8

TABLE 7
Scoring Criteria for
Figure Ascendence

Ascendance		ASCSEL	ASCMOM	ASCDAD
Head in bottom	1/8	1	1	1
Head in bottom	1/4	2	2	2
Head in bottom	1/2	3	3	3
Head in top	1/2	4	4	4
Head in top	1/4	5	5	5
Head in top	1/8	6	6	6

TABLE 8
Scoring Criteria for
Figure Communication Level

Communication	COMSEL	COMMOM	COMDAD
Sleeping	0	0	0
Watching	1	1	1
Listening	2	2	2
Talking	3	3	3
Playing with (person)	4	4	4
Touching (person)	5	5	5
Holding (person)	6	6	6

TABLE 9
Scoring Criteria for
Figure Cooperation

Cooperation	COOPSE	COOPMO	COOPDA
No cooperation	0	0	0
Working	1	1	1
Helping	2	2	2
Playing (together)	3	3	3
Working (together)	4	4	4

TABLE 10
Scoring Criteria for
Figure Direction

Figure Direction	FACSEL	FACMOM	FACDAD
Facing out of drawing	1	1	1
Facing away from major figures	2	2	2
Facing into drawing	3	3	3
Facing major figures	4	4	4

TABLE 11
Scoring Criteria for
Masochism

Masochism	MASSEL	MASMOM	MASDAD
No Masochism	0	0	0
Smoking	1	1	1
Being hit	2	2	2
Being hurt	3	3	3
Being kicked	4	4	4
Being cut	5	5	5
Being burned	6	6	6
Being shot	7	7	7
Being killed	8	8	8

TABLE 12
Scoring Criteria for
Figure Narcissism

Narcissism	NARSEL	NARMOM	NARDAD
No Narcissism	0	0	0
Dressing	1	1	1
Combing	2	2	2
Grooming	3	3	3
Drinking	4	4	4
Looking in a mirror	5	5	5

TABLE 13
Scoring Criteria for
Figure Nurturing

Nurturance	NURSEL	NURMOM	NURDAD
No Nurturing	0	0	0
Planting	1	1	1
Helping	2	2	2
Grooming	3	3	3
Cooking	4	4	4
Touching	5	5	5
Holding	6	6	6
Feeding	7	7	7

TABLE 14
Scoring Criteria for
Figure Sadism

Sadism	SADSEL	SADMOM	SADDAD
No Sadism	0	0	0
Hitting	1	1	1
Fighting	2	2	2
Hurting	3	3	3
Kicking	4	4	4
Biting	5	5	5
Burning	6	6	6
Shooting	7	7	7
Killing	8	8	8

TABLE 15
Scoring Criteria for
Figure Tension

Tension	TENSEL	TENMOM	TENDAD
No Tension	0	0	0
Slipping	1	1	1
Hanging	2	2	2
Falling	3	3	3

TABLE 16
Scoring Criteria for
Body

Body	BODSEL	BODMOM	BODDAD
Absent	0	0	0
Head only	1	1	1
Head and Neck	2	2	2
Head, Neck, Torso	3	3	3
Head, Neck, Torso, Leg	4	4	4
Complete	5	5	5

TABLE 17
Scoring Criteria for
Roots (size of feet)

Roots	FEESEL	FEEMOM	FEEDAD
Feet Missing	0	0	0
Feet on Wheels (i.e. car, bike skates)	1	1	1
Feet $\frac{1}{4}$ or less length of leg	2	2	2
Feet over $\frac{1}{4}$ to $\frac{1}{2}$ length of leg	3	3	3
Feet 3/4 or more length of leg	4	4	4

TABLE 18
Scoring Criteria for
Size of Figures (millimeters)

Size	SIZSEL	SIZMOM	SIZDAD

TABLE 19
Scoring Criteria for
Arm Length

Arm Length	ARMSEL	ARMMOM	ARMDAD
Arms Missing	0	0	0
0 to 1/8 length of body	1	1	1
1/8 to 1/4 length of body	2	2	2
1/4 to 3/8 length of body	3	3	3
3/8 to 1/2 length of body	4	4	4
1/2 to 3/4 length of body	5	5	5
Greater than 3/4 length of body	6	6	6

TABLE 20
Scoring Criteria for
Eyes

Eyes	EYESEL	EYEMOM	EYEDAD
Absent	0	0	0
Eyes but no pupil showing	1	1	1
complete (eyes plus pupil)	2	2	2

TABLE 21
Scoring Criteria for
Facial Expression

Expression	FACEXS	FACESM	FACEXP
Very Friendly	1	1	1
Friendly	2	2	2
Neutral	3	3	3
Unfriendly	4	4	4
Very Unfriendly	5	5	5

TABLE 22
Scoring Criteria for
Face

Face	FACSEL	FACMOM	FACDAD
absent	0	0	0
eyes only	1	1	1
eyes & nose or mouth	2	2	2
eyes, nose, and mouth	3	3	3

TABLE 23
Scoring Criteria for
Number of Sibs Present

0
1
2
3
4
5
6
7
8 and above

TABLE 24
Scoring Criteria for
Parent Missing

Missing	PARMSM	PARMSD	PARMSB
Mother	1		
Father		1	
Both			1

TABLE 25
Scoring Criteria for
Teeth Present

Teeth	TEESEL	TEEMOM	TEEDAD
Absent	0	0	0
Present	1	1	1

TABLE 27
Orientation Between Figures
(Score 1 if figure is facing. Example: ORDM;
score 1 if dad is facing mom. ORDS;
score 1 if dad is facing self, etc.)

Figure Orientation
ORDM
ORDS
ORMD
ORMS
ORSM
ORSD

TABLE 26
Scoring Criteria for
Number of Barriers

	BARRSM	BARRSD	BARRMD
Number of Barriers between			

TABLE 28
Scoring Criteria for
Styles

Style	Absence of Style	Mildly Suggestive	Moderately Suggestive	Strongly Suggestive	Meets all Criteria
Compart	0	1	2	3	4
Edging	0	1	2	3	4
Encaps	0	1	2	3	4
Folcom	0	1	2	3	4
Lin Bot	0	1	2	3	4
Lin Top	0	1	2	3	4
Undlif	0	1	2	3	4
Birdiv	0	1	2	3	4

TABLE 29
Scoring Criteria for
Like-To-Live-In-Family (LILIF)

	Definitely Not	Probably Not	Neutral	Probably	Definitely
Like-To-Live in KFD Family	0	1	2	3	4

IV. CLINICAL AND COMPUTER INTERPRETATIONS
   OF A K-F-D

Drawing 41, a D-A-P, was done by 12-year-old Dan. The D-A-P portrays a rather sinister-appearing adult – well-groomed but with a hard, unsmiling expression. When asked who the person was, Dan said he didn't know. Later in an interview, Dan's mother said the D-A-P looked just like her brother, a car salesman Dan admired.

DRAWING 41

Dan's stepfather is an alcoholic with a 14-year-old son from his first marriage. Dan was a product of the mother's first marriage. The two younger sibs came from the union of the K-F-D depicting mom and dad, seen in Dan's K-F-D, Drawing 42. Drawing 42 may be analyzed from an artistic or from a scientific viewpoint. Let's try both.

A. Artistic Analysis of K-F-D 42

The dominant feature of the drawing appears to be the dirt thrown by a faceless alcoholic stepdad the length of the drawing but ending in the direction of the self. The scribbling all over the stepdad figure reflects anxiety invested in this menacing figure. The faceless subordinate rescuing mother is racing toward the stepfather. The K-F-D-S is vigilant in "eyeing" the mother and touching her with the competitive energy symbolized in the football. Dan is far from the dad but close to the mom.

The older stepbrother, a bully, is hanging (tension) over the K-F-D-S. The little brother is enlarged, ascendent, and close to the dad. The sister is viewed as ascendent and close to mom. The swirling K-F-D gives a feeling of tension. Only Dan has a "seeing" eye and appears to see the other family members vaguely and "through a glass darkly."

One would not want to live in this family unless the dad stopped throwing dirt, messing up the family, and threatening everyone. In actuality, the mother had just developed enough strength to insist the father seek help with Alcoholics Anonymous. The dad had agreed. Dan's view of the family through the K-F-D served as a spark to the mother in her desire to help the family.

B. Computer Analysis of K-F-D 42

Table 30 is a summary of the raw drawing scores for the Actions, Styles, Figure characteristics, position, distances, and barriers in K-F-D 42.

In reviewing column 1, we see a 3 score for SADDAS, which suggests a SADISTIC DAD. The figure characteristics in column 2 reveal the mother's size, SIZMOM, larger than dad, SIZDAD, with the self, SIZSEL, smaller than either. Column 3 suggests that the self is closer to the mother DISTSM (15mm) and more distant from the dad DISTSD (81mm); the mom is seen closer to the dad, DISTMD (4mm).

DRAWING 42

Little Brother (5) Jumping

Step Dad shoveling dirt

Mom skiing

Sister (8) balleting

Step-Brother on trapeze (14)

Tee

(12) Self kicking football

TABLE 30
Raw Computer Variables for K-F-D 42

ACTIONS			FIGURE CHARACTERISTICS			POSITION, DISTANCE AND BARRIERS			STYLES			LIKE TO LIVE IN FAMILY (LILIF)	
Variables	X	SD	Variables	X	SD	Variables	X	SD	Variables	X	SD	X	SD
ACTDAD	7		ARMDAD	4		ASCDAD	4		COMPART	0			
ACTMOM	5		ARMMOM	4		ASCMOM	3		EDGING	0			
ACTSEL	5		ARMSEL	3		ASCSEL	3		ENCAPS	0			
COMDAD	0		BODDAD	5		BARRMD	1		FOLCOM	0			
COMMOM	0		BODMOM	5		BARRSD	3		LINBOT	0			
COMSEL	0		BODSEL	5		BARRSM	1		LINTOP	0			
COOPDA	0		EYEDAD	0		DIRDAD	1		UNDLIF	4			
COOPMO	0		EYEMOM	0		DIRMOM	4		BIRDIV	0			
COOPSE	0		EYESEL	2		DIRSEL	4						
MASDAD	0		FACDAD	0		DISTMD	4mm						
MASMOM	0		FACMOM	0		DISTSD	81mm						
MASSEL	2		FACSEL	2		DISTSM	15mm						
NARDAD	0		FACEXD	0		ORDM	0						
NARMOM	0		FACEXM	0		ORDS	1						
NARSEL	0		FACEXS	0		ORMD	0						
NURDAD	0		FEEDAD	3		ORMS	0						
NURMOM	0		FEEMOM	4		ORSM	1						
NURSEL	0		FEESEL	3		ORSD	1						
SADDAD	3		NOSIBS	4									
SADMOM	0		PARMSM	0									
SADSEL	0		PARMSD	0									
TENDAD	1		PARMSB	0									
TENMOM	1		SEX	M									
TENSEL	1		SIZDAD	50mm									
			SIZMOM	56mm									
			SIZSEL	42mm									
			TEEDAD	0									
			TEEMOM	0									
			TEESEL	0									

V. INSTRUCTIONS FOR JUDGING
KINETIC FAMILY DRAWINGS (K-F-Ds) AND STYLES

The drawings are to be analyzed as to their relationship to eight style dimensions. For every given style, each drawing must be rated along a continuum from 0 to 4 (see below).

0	1	2	3	4
Complete absence of style	mildly suggests the style	moderately suggests the style	strongly suggests the style	meets all criteria for the style

For example: If a drawing fully meets the criteria for a specific style, it is scored at the maximum point along the above scale – 4. When the drawing does not meet fully the criteria of a style but resembles it to some degree, it is to be rated accordingly on the scale. The rater should be thoroughly familiar with the criteria of the eight styles before making any judgments.

It is exceptionally rare to find a single drawing exhibiting characteristics of every style. However, it is likely that many drawings will manifest little or no style whatsoever.

Experience with previous raters has shown that it is extremely IMPORTANT to:

1) *Be conservative* (if doubtful, score toward the lower end)
2) *Review criteria often* (after rating a number of drawings, one has the tendency to ignore the written criteria, feeling one has a good grasp of them – this has been an illusion in many cases)
3) *Watch for carelessness*

NOTE: The above scoring instructions are essentially from the Doctoral Dissertation of John McPhee (57). The following pages 88, 89, 91, 92, 93 and 94 are based on McPhee's work (57).

A. Style – Compartmentalization (COMPART)

This style is characterized by the intentional separation of family figures through the use of *lining*.

Examples Rated 4

Examples Rated 0

B. Style – Edging

Edging is revealed by the subject who places *all* the family figures on the perimeter of the paper in a rectangular style. Occasionally this style results in various figures being "cut off." At least two sides of the 8½ X 11 paper must have family members positioned along the edges (with the edges serving as bottoms to the figures); otherwise the drawing is NOT scored as Edging and is given a rating of 0. Generally children must turn the paper in several directions in order to produce this style.

Examples Rated 4

Examples Rated 0

C. Style – Encapsulation (ENCAPS)

This style consists of encapsulating one or more figures. The figure may be enclosed by an object such as a jump rope, car, airplane, etc. or by lines. If the entire drawing is separated into compartments, COMPART will be scored rather than ENCAPS.

Examples Rated 4

Examples Rated 0

90

D. Style – Folding Compartmentalization (FOLCOM)

Folding compartmentalization is perhaps the easiest style to score. The style is manifested by children who fold the paper into segments and place individual figures in the compartments.

Examples Rated 4

Example Rated 0

E. Style – Lining on the Bottom (LINBOT)

This style (for a rating of 4) consists of *more than one line covering the entire bottom* of the drawing. If the lining is not at the very bottom of the whole picture (drawing), then LINBOT is rated 0. The wider the strip at the bottom and the more intense the shading, the more confident one can be of his judgment.

Examples Rated 4

Underlining individuals not
lining on the bottom

Lining not across the entire
bottom and only one line

Examples Rated 0

F. Style – Lining at the Top (LINTOP)

Drawings designated as having this style have more than one line extending across the entire top of the K-F-D (for a rating of 4). The wider the strip and the more intense the shading, the more certain one can be of categorizing the drawing as LINTOP.

Examples Rated 4

Examples Rated 0

G. Style – Underlining Individual Figures (UNDLIF)

This style is quite similar to Lining on the Bottom but differs in that the lining is immediately below an upright (standing) individual (or several individuals). At least two (2) lines (or the obvious repetition of the same line) must appear under the whole person if UNDLIF is to be scored as 4. (Sitting or lying on a common, natural object is NOT scored as Underlining and is rated as 0.)

Examples Rated 4

sitting on a chair

lying

lining on
the bottom

individual
extends below
the underlining.

Examples Rated 0

H. Style – Bird's Eye View (BIRDIV)

This style is present when a bird's eye or aerial view is present in the K-F-D. The style is manifested when tops of all people, objects, tables, etc. are seen from above.

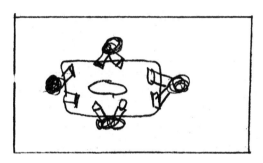

Example Rated 4

Example Rated 0

VI. K-F-D GRID

A grid made of tracing paper marked off in millimeters has proven useful in obtaining certain K-F-D data. By superimposing the grid over a K-F-D, a number of measurements may be made.

The grid may be of help in obtaining the measurements of the self and other K-F-D figures. The distance of the self from the other figures is also an important drawing variable.

The location of the self and the other figures on the grid may also be of interest. For example, conditions such as "superiority" or "inferiority" complex may be defined in terms of the size of the self and placement on the grid.

Such measurements may be of value in studying the individual as his or her own control or in studying the differences between intra- or inter-cultural variables.

Much critical research is still needed. For example, new stepwise regression equations might be developed using a wide variety of variables.

Common sense suggests that high scores indicating very friendly faces (FACES, FACEM, FACED) + complete bodies (BODSEL, BODMOM, BODDAD) + nourishing parents (NURDAD, NURMOM) + rootedness (FEESEL, FEEMOM, FEEDAD) related to 0 scores on barriers (BARRMD, BARRSD, BARRSM) might yield an equation highly correlated with self-growth, self-worth, etc.

VII. WAYS OF VIEWING K-F-Ds.

Before looking at the clinical aspects of drawings, I would like to share two simplistic ways of view K-F-Ds.

In Figure 3, #3, for example, the causal observer simply sees a picture of members of a family with the drawer depicted sitting behind a desk. Through the technique of deleting content, the clinician is able to ask the significant question – why is the area below the drawer's waist omitted (#4)?

Figure 3. View Figures Deleting Content

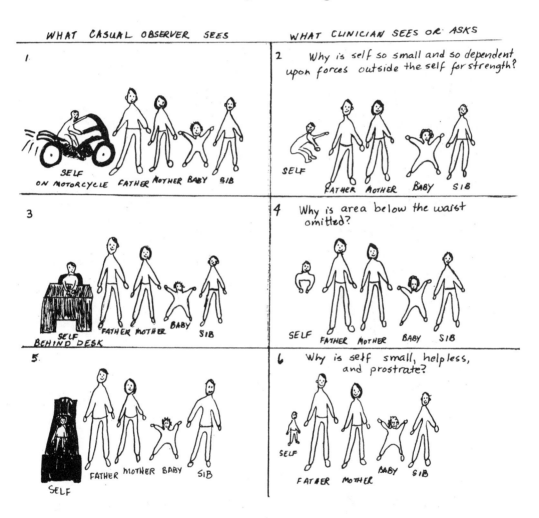

In Figure 4, #7, the causal observer sees a domestic family scene. Through the technique of deleting figures, the clinician focuses on the cleaning utensils and poses the question – what is the significance of the overemphasis on cleaning (#8)?

Although we may struggle to make drawing interpretations a science, much of it remains an art. Chapter 5 begins an attempt to deal with advanced interpretation of the K-F-D.

Figure 4: View Content Deleting Figures

CHAPTER 5

IDENTIFICATION WITHIN THE FAMILY FOR BETTER OR FOR WORSE

In the process of identification, the self grows by internalizing the feelings and values of the parental figures. If the parental feelings and values internalized are positive and growth-producing, the child may develop a healthy, positive self-image. If the parental feelings and values are negative and destructive, the child may develop an unhealthy negative self-image.

I. PARENTAL IDENTIFICATION LEADING TO POSITIVE SELF-IMAGE

Consider, for example, Drawing 43 done by Eric, age 5. Eric is close to the mother and is holding hands with her, while dad is near the younger brother. There is a closeness in the drawing, however, with no separation and no boxing-in of figures or any other way of isolating members. One senses a warmth in the family, even though jealousy about the father being near the brother is suggested by the underlining of the father. Eric should be able to identify with the parents, who are close, loving, and accepting.

DRAWING 43

MOM

DAD

SELF (5)

BROTHER

In Drawing 44, Janey, age 7, views the family as a happy one. The central theme in the very middle and top of the picture is the harmony of the music. Even the dogs are happy, as is Janey, who looks like the mother and is close to her. In this family, people are helping each other and there is a total harmony suggested by the closeness and the central theme of music and well-being. Janey has identified with her mother.

DRAWING 44

Acting brother up

Going to eat egg

Big brother (11)

Brother

Dad

splash

wishing well

getting water

mom

Flower

Puppy

me

Dog

In Drawing 45, 6½-year-old Luanne also appears dominant in the family. In contrast to Mike, who is winning the battle to control mother, Luanne is in the process of winning the battle to control father. She is standing next to him and has her balloon, a symbol of ascendence. However, she has a dress like her mother's and is quite like her in appearance, only stronger with a larger head – suggesting that Luanne has a very good opinion of herself. She is quite capable of not only identifying with the mother in her feminine role but also with her need for ascendence in the family, a role she copies from the large father. Luanne is androgynous, combining the best of the feminine and masculine components in her family and identifying with these.

DRAWING 45

Mary weeding the flowers

shovel

Balloon

6½

"Bad guy!"

Ha not to "Bad-a eat in the table"

In Drawing 46, 7½-year-old Gloria shows a family in which mother and father are facing the children. There are few boundaries and expressions are happy. The overall impression from Drawing 43 is one of a family where the parents are facing the children, are ascendent, and are there to meet their needs. They are strong parents and the children respect and identify with their strength.

DRAWING 46

SISTER (1)
DUSTING TV

SISTER
WRITING
in book (4)

MOM "STANDING"

WATCHING
TV

SISTER
(1)

BROTHER (3)

BROTHER (3)
COLORING

COLORING ME (4) 7½

NEWS

DAD

Eleven-year-old Ray produced Drawing 47. This type of drawing, usually done by boys, in which the family is playing ball, is often associated with children willing to engage in constructive competitive activity. Ray seems to thrive on competition to gain ascendence in the family constellation. He has identified with dad and is "willing to play ball."

DRAWING 47

Me (11)

DaD

Mom

sister (13)

BROTHER (5)

BROTHER (2)

TEDDY (8)

family playing Ball

In Drawing 48, 16-year-old George depicts a more complicated picture. He appears to compete with the older brother, who is larger and dominant. One notes, however, that George repeats himself and is close to the father, who is "giving" him the pants in the family. The pants seem to be the symbol of manhood to George. The father is smiling and benevolent and facing his son. The strong, nurturant mother is witnessing the transaction and perhaps giving her approval. Again, the drawing suggests a closeness to the father and a willingness to "follow in his footsteps" and to copy him by accepting the gift of manhood.

DRAWING 48

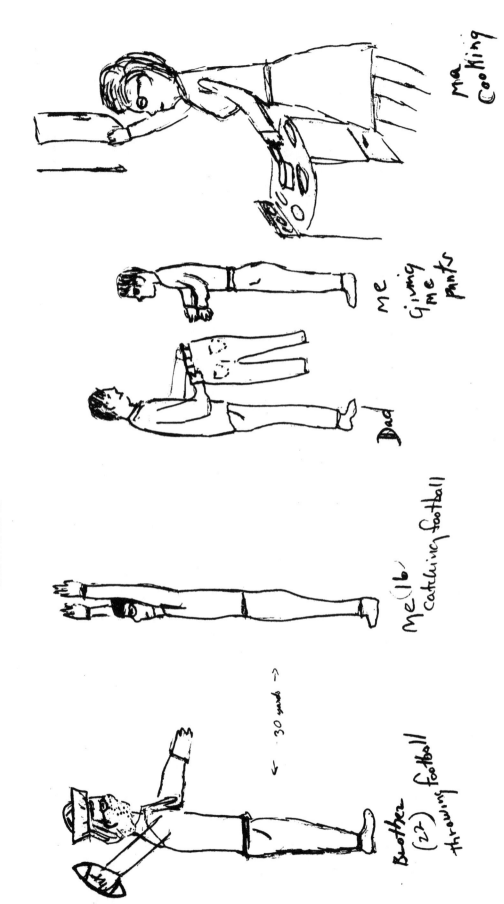

II. PARENTAL IDENTIFICATION LEADING
TO NEGATIVE SELF-IMAGE

In Drawing 49, 6½-year-old Mike shows a very different way to identify. Note that both he and his father have a black eye and a very large arm. Mike is in the process of struggling with the father for dominance in the family. Mike seems to be winning. He is at the top and actually is somewhat larger than the father, although the father's arm may be larger. The son apparently has identified with the father's aggressiveness and, because of the son's strength, he is able to imitate the father's behavior and to internalize his aggressive ways. Mike has identified with the father for better or for worse.

Mike- fighting
has black eye

6½

mommy
making dinner

Brian 1
throwing toys around

Lisa 6
fighting with Mike
and playing with
toys in bedroom

Daddy fighting
with Mike.
has black eye

DRAWING 49

Fifteen-year-old Mary produced K-F-D 50. The tremendous guilt felt by Mary is indicated by all family members pointing their fingers at her. She is looking for approval, in a downcast way, from the father. Mary directs anger toward her sister, which is perhaps the cause of the parental and family chastisement. While Mary does identify with parental values, they seem to be of a highly moralistic nature. At this stage of Mary's life, she feels guilt through her identification with parental rules which she has broken.

DRAWING 50

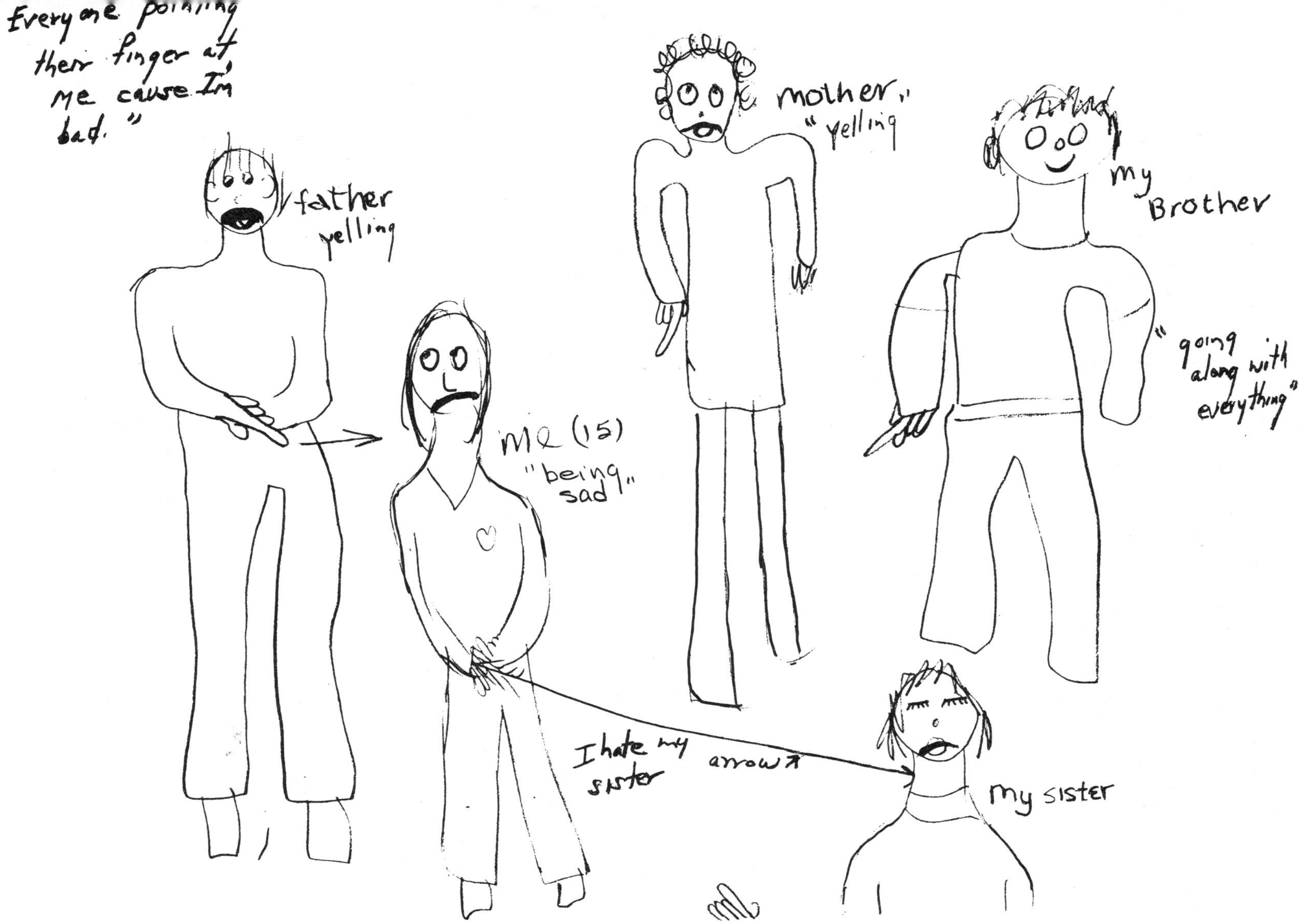

my Brother

"going with along everything"

my sister

mother, "yelling"

I hate my sister

arrows

Me (15) "being sad"

father yelling

Everyone pointing ther finger at me. cause I'm bad."

Drawing 51 by 14-year-old Jan suggests another form of identification. Everyone in this family is working. The father appears to be immobilized. The mother asserts her dominance with a belt. Jan has turned her back on the situation, but still places herself in the family. One suspects that she does identify with the family, even though she may have a "Cinderella" complex. This is the type of girl, who, when she grows up and is under pressure, may tend to obsessively clean as atonement.

Jan seems to have incorporated the values of the mother. She puts herself in a central position to the family. She is angry with the pressures but seems to grudgingly accept them as some older children, particularly older daughters, do. Throughout life she may feel responsibilities for the other members of the family, but these will be mixed with ambivalence. Thus, she may be more interested in cleaniness in her house than in interpersonal values. The lack of face and feet in their K-F-D-S suggests that Jan may move on as soon as feasible.

DRAWING 51

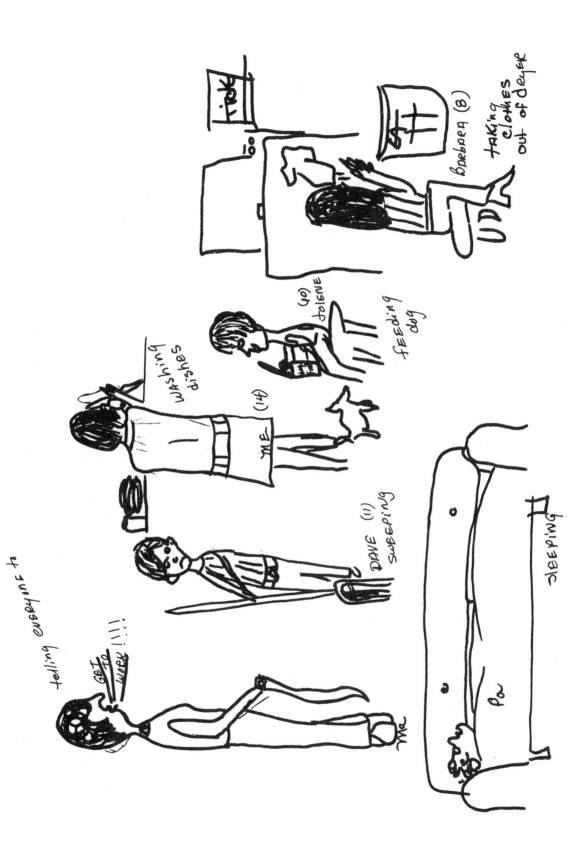

In Drawing 52, 10-year-old Ed shows a more subtle form of iden-tification. He and the father both have smiles on their faces, in contrast to the mother's somewhat anguished look. This mother is dominant, as indicated by her ascendent position. However, the boy is close to the father and the father is of more importance to him, as indicated by dad's size. The mother is trying to make Ed stand up, but he is "lying down." This struggle seems to please the father and one suspects that the boy is acting out the father's own desire to struggle with the ascen-dent mother. The identification the boy feels for the father, then, is perhaps contructive in their relationship but destructive in regard to the mother. The passive resistance Ed shows her may carry over into school or life; when women teachers expect something from him, he may become passively resistant and refuse to comply or will comply in a way which may result in failure. Of course, if Ed eventually marries, this "game" may continue with his wife.

DRAWING 52

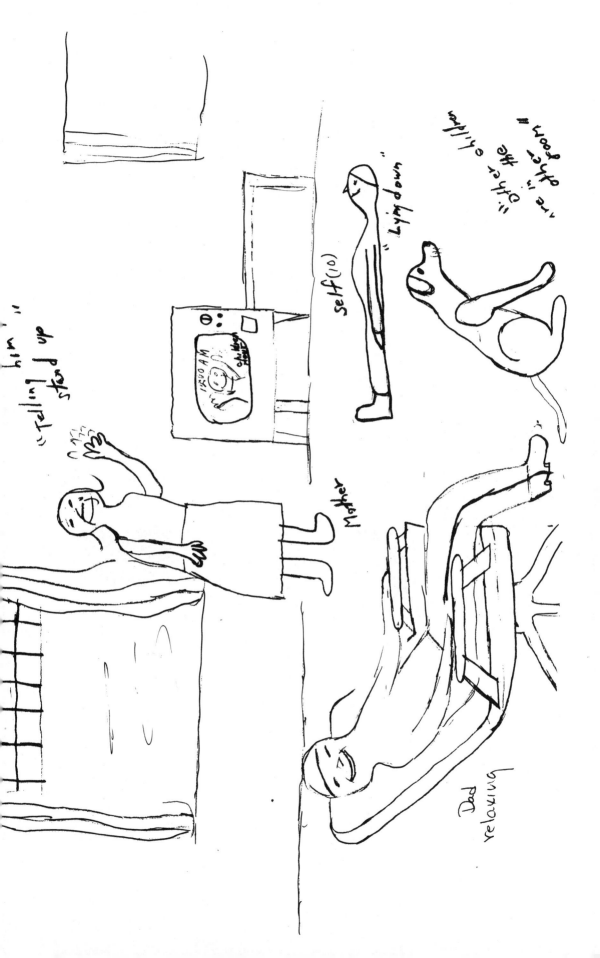

Drawing 53, by 10-year-old Boris, shows a more passive identification. He is "listening" to dad and is close to him. However, Boris is also in a box. The shading suggests a great deal of anxiety associated with his own body and perhaps with the obsessive-compulsive design drawn instead of his sister. While Boris is still listening to the father, one has the feeling that he may be withdrawing into a shell and perhaps the father should put down his horn and interact with his son so Boris may complete his identification process and continue to "listen" to Dad.

In many families the child does not complete the identification process. Some determined children will not give up and try perhaps for a lifetime to gain parental approval and thus complete their identification. Many children give up trying to identify with the parents and look outside the family for identification or simply give up.

Dad "playing horn"

ME (10) "Listening to dad"

sister "can't finish"

DRAWING 53

CHAPTER 6

INABILITY TO IDENTIFY
WITHIN THE NUCLEAR FAMILY

For a variety of reasons children may not be able to identify within the nuclear family. The child may then seek identification with a substitute family or person, identify with power or fantasy substitutes, become narcissistic and fall in love with him/herself, or become depressed or suicidal. Here are some of the common situations associated with inability to identify in a nuclear family.

I. THE SEPARATED CHILD

A. Divorce

At the time of a divorce, all members of the family are under a great deal of stress and extreme emotional conditions. It is at such a time that wise decisions are difficult to reach.

From the child's point of view, she/he often feels some loyalty toward a parent, even though he/she may actually feel much resentment toward the same parent. At times, children feel very sorry for a parent who is ill or has a chronic problem such as alcoholism. If asked to make a choice they may pick this parent, although at a deeper emotional level they may well reject the parent and may enter into period of confusion and emotional deprivation.

B. Which Parent Should the Separated
    Child Live With?

Which parent should the child live with? Where does she/he feel
warm, or loved, or needed?

Even very young children can depict an unstable family climate in
their simple but very effective way.

For example, Jimmy, age 4, who produced the D-A-P, Drawing
54, was living with the true mother, who had remarried. He often
visited the true father, who had also remarried. When Jimmy was
asked to draw a picture of his family with his mother, he produced
Drawing 55. It is a simple drawing, but it effectively shows the
closeness of Jimmy to his mother and the somewhat less important
stepfather.

DRAWING 54

Mom

me

step-dad

DRAWING 55

On the same day, when asked to draw a picture of the family with the true father, Jimmy produced Drawing 56. In the drawing, Jimmy put windows which "get breaked" and he has windows crashing on dad's head. He effectively places himself in a box away from the parents, both of whom are getting hurt, but he is safe.

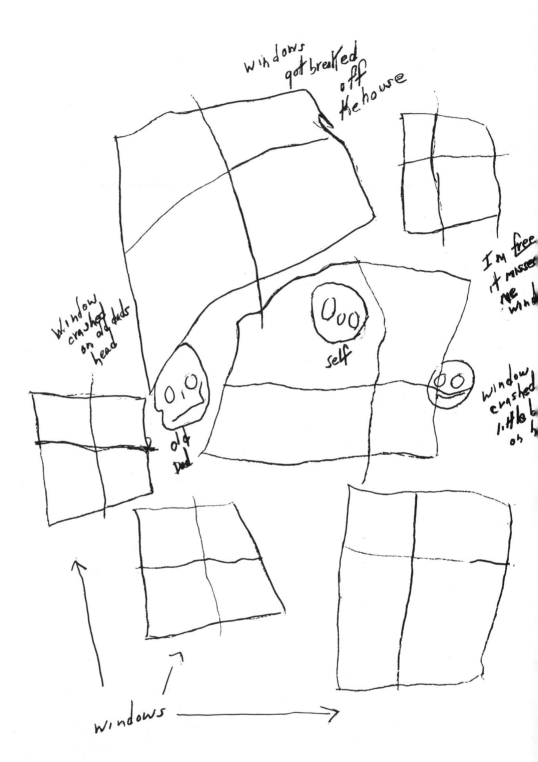

windows got breaked off the house

Window crashed on old dads head

old Dad

self

I'm free it misses me wind

window crashed little b on h

windows ⟶

DRAWING 56

Two weeks later, Jimmy was reevaluated and the instructions were repeated to draw everybody in the mother's family in action. He produced Drawing 57. Again, he shows a relatively tranquil family in which there is closeness – no barriers and no violence.

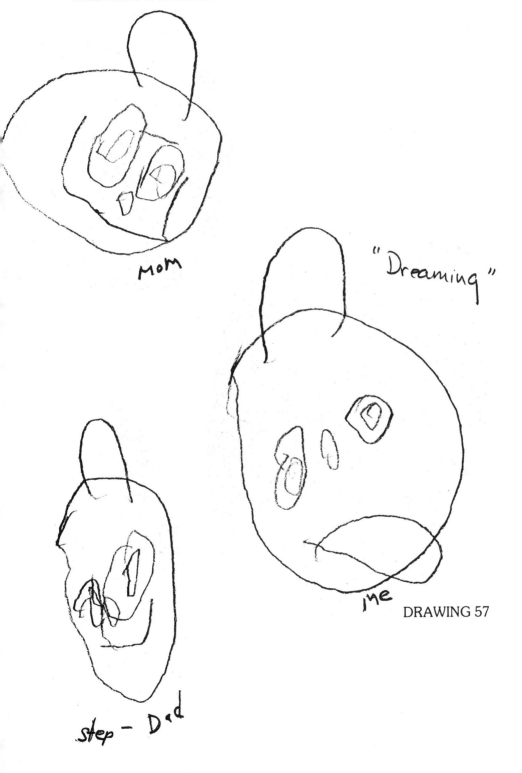

MoM

"Dreaming"

me

step – Dad

DRAWING 57

When asked to repeat a K-F-D of the father's family, he first heavily shaded the top of Drawing 58 and said, "This is wood breaking." The wood "smacked" the father and stepmother on their heads but "missed me." We note that the K-F-D-S has only a partial face. Rocks are also falling in the drawing and the mood of violence continues in the drawings of the family of the true father.

When we review Jimmy's D-A-P, we see the hat on top of the head. The hat is present in the drawings with the true mother but not in the family with the true father. Jimmy's D-A-P appears to represent a wish fulfillment to be with his mother.

Even in 4-year-old Jimmy's depiction of the family, we see him using compartmentalization. We also see a partially faceless self in the K-F-D with the true father.

These drawings proved helpful in having the boy's true father see that Jimmy felt a violence in his family which was detrimental to Jimmy.

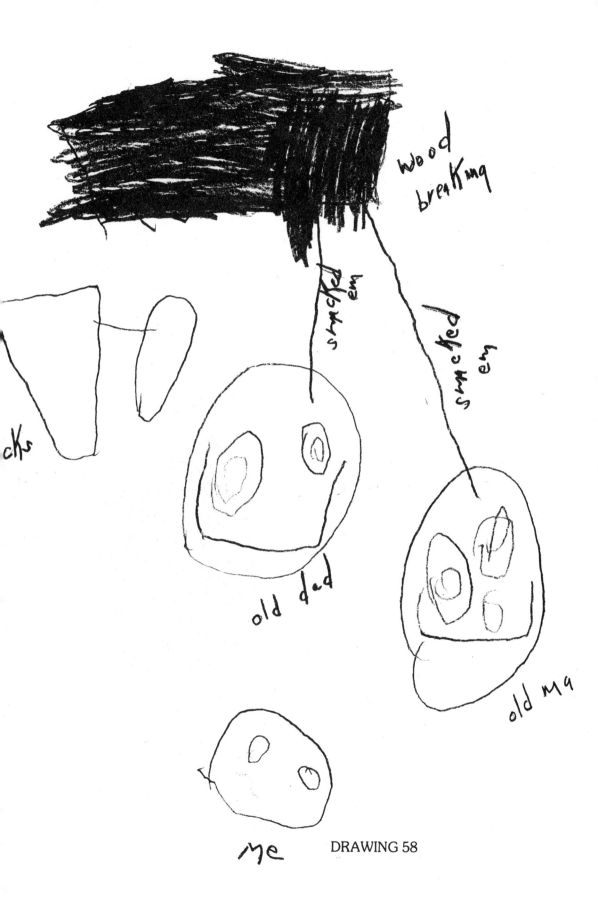

wood
breakting

cke

old dad

old ma

me   DRAWING 58

Sometimes, constant arguing by parents in the midst of a divorce forces children to shut them out and turn away, as depicted by 10-year-old Tom in Drawing 59.

DRAWING 59

C. Which Culture Should the Separated Child Live In?

In Drawing 60 by 12-year-old Michael, we see his depiction of his "city" family. His parents were divorced. The mother was a full-blooded American Indian; the father was "white." Mother had gone back to the reservation and father had custody of Michael. The stark coldness of K-F-D 60 reflects Michael's loneliness in the city.

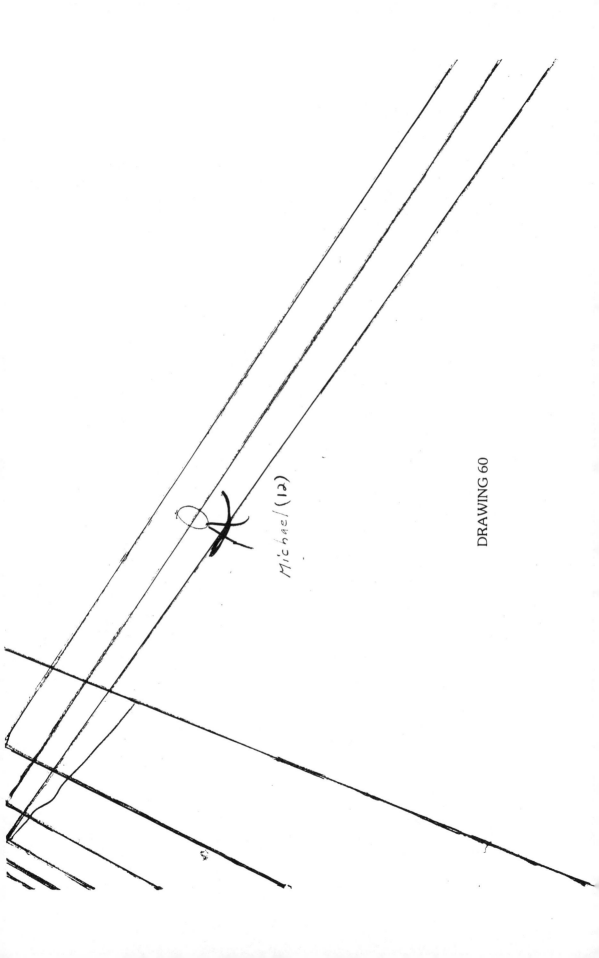

Michael (12)

DRAWING 60

When asked to draw a K-F-D living with the mother on the reservation, Michael produced Drawing 61.

The intense sun in K-F-D 61 bathes the reservation with warmth, reflecting Michael's feelings of warmth and acceptance in this Indian culture and family. The K-F-D was instrumental in convincing the father to allow Michael to move to the reservation rather than become an alcoholic, as had an older brother brought up in the coldness of the city, so simply communicated in K-F-D 60.

DRAWING 61

FOSTER AND ADOPTIVE HOME PLACEMENT – Finding appropriate homes for foster children is a grave responsibility. Often, decisions as to placement and separation of foster children can be critical in terms of the particular foster child's ability to develop normally and became a meaningful member of society.

There are often interviews with the children, but because of their age and the great stress they are under they are often unable to make rational decisions. Interview material with the children can be quite misleading. For example, some children feel that no matter how terrible the home is they have a responsibility to the parent and are often dragged down with such parents.

GROUP HOME VERSUS FOSTER HOME – During adolescence, but sometimes much earlier, there is a real question regarding the benefits of a group home versus a foster home placement. K-F-Ds can often give information useful in helping to make such a decision.

Drawing 62 is by 13-year-old Tom. The mother had married a year prior to the drawing. A 15-year-old daughter had previously been placed in a foster home.

Because of many stresses within the present marriage, the mother and caseworker were seeking foster home placement for Tom. We note the extreme immaturity of this drawing for a boy of 13. Tom is facing and close to the mother, and they are both eating. The stepfather's chair has been placed some distance from the table and, despite his long arms, he will have difficulty reaching the food. The style is lining at the bottom (LINBOT) and the mother is heavily shaded. Despite the babyish relation to the mother, Tom's head resembles that of the stepfather with whom Tom apparently tries to identify. Tom is still struggling with identification and growing up within the family. If he is placed outside the home, Tom would probably do much better in a foster home than a group home.

DRAWING 62

In contrast to Tom's immature K-F-D-S, 14-year-old Shirley is not working on family dynamics. Shirley is a runaway and being considered for foster or group home placement.

Drawing 63 shows Shirley depicting her K-F-D-S outside the home – encapsulated with her group. The K-F-D suggests Shirley is ready for and might do much better in a group home.

DRAWING 63

pounds - reward gets a new wardrobe.
billy I lost 25 pounds I need a new wardrobe
DAD - fishing
A Fish
ME(14) - having
My mom & dad letting me go somewhere and not having to be worried
CONVENTION
me
Mom
Bus
GOING away
June - getting a new doll.
a new doll!
DAN - watching T.V.
super man!
T.V.

FOSTER HOME OR OWN HOME – Eight-year-old Tom had been in a foster home for two years with two of his brothers. His mother had remarried and there was a question of whether the boys should be returned to the mother or stay in the foster home. Tom was asked to make a K-F-D depicting his foster family and he made K-F-D 64.

DRAWING 64

The blank faces and missing foster parents reflect Tom's lack of identification in this setting. Tom was asked to make a K-F-D following a three-day visit with the true mother and stepdad.

Two brothers and the parents have a face. The K-F-D-S still has no face. However the closeness to the stepdad and the stepdad's complete face suggest identification with him is possible in contrast to the lonely, faceless K-F-D-S in the foster home. Tom has more chances for self-growth in the family with the true mother and needs some stability in a growth-conducive environment in order to catch up.

DRAWING 65

Brother going over to chair to
Danny (11)

Eddie sitting
(12) Brother

walking
over to
chair
Dad

Self (8)

Mike
Jim

mom walking to chair

THE REJECTING PARENT – Sometimes a child is not separated but is rejected within the nuclear family.

In Drawing 66 by 10-year-old Sally, we see the beginning of identification outside the family. In this drawing, the mother has her back turned to Sally. Sally is identical to her 8-year-old friend, Julie, and they are out of the house going to the store. Dad also seems busy with his newspaper. This little girl often refers to her mother as the "witch" and perhaps the TV program the 13-year-old brother is watching has something to do with the dynamics within the family from Sally's point of view. Sally finds identification with her friend more satisfying than with mother at this point in her life.

DRAWING 66

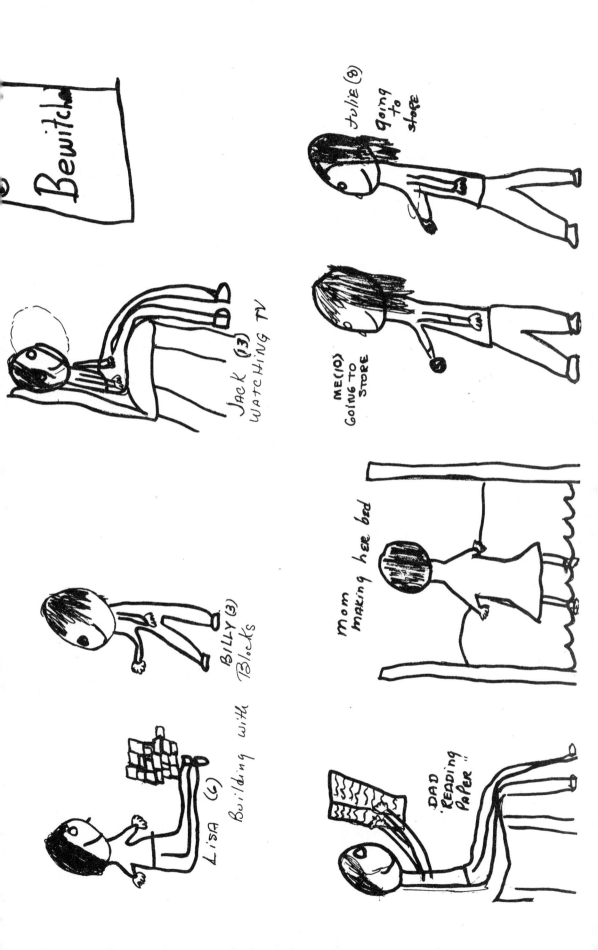

THE TUNING-OUT PARENT – Some parents are capable of tuning out their children and ignoring them.

Nine-and-a-half-year-old Gary in Drawing 67 is ignored by the father and mother. The father has a favorite, his older boy. Gary's K-F-D-S is a pathetic-looking, isolated figure. The older sister is the only one he sees clearly in the family. He faces and looks at her hoping he can get some warmth from her. The lack of identification with the males in the family and the pathetic feelings of inadequacy portrayed by Gary's self-portrait suggest a poor self-image and trouble for Gary in finding his identity in the future.

Mom

Dad

Brother

gary 9½

sister 19

In Drawing 68 by 9-year-old Eric, we see Eric encapsulated with his 3-year-old sister. At this stage of his life, he appears to have identified with her. He has been having problems with soiling and wetting the bed.

Eric has had trouble with school adjustment and with reading. He feels alienated from the parents. The father is involved with watching football on TV. Eric is not proficient in sports. The mother is sitting next to the 7-year-old brother, who is reading. Thus, Eric feels closer to the 3-year-old sister. To date, he has not been able to identify with the parents, especially the highly academically-oriented mother.

DAD "WATCHING TV"

Mom "book turned"

Brother (7) "READING"

ME (9)

Little sister (3)

arm wrestling on Rug

DRAWING 68

WORKAHOLIC PARENT – In Drawing 69, 8-year-old Tom is facing toward the father and the family. However, there is no father – only an office building. From Tom's point of view, the father has been swallowed by his work. The boy seems ready to play ball with dad and is looking toward the building. One wonders how long Tom will wait for the father to pay attention to him. The mother's expression also suggests that she has some of the same hopeless feelings as do the faceless brother and sister.

DRAWING 69

SISTER (12)

BROTHER (3)

crys

dad
working
all day
in his
office

Playing
sports

strike one
"ME"
(8)

mom
cleaning
the house

Five-year-old Jenny in Drawing 70 has a working mother. Jenny made her K-F-D with her mother standing next to her. She then erased mother. She drew the father and sister in the home, but the mother is missing. This mother has worked since Jenny was a year old. Jenny has a very vague idea of her mother and thus will have difficulty in truly identifying with her. The search for the mother may continue throughout Jenny's life. Note the lining at the bottom of the K-F-D reflecting Jenny's concern for stability and rootedness.

DRAWING 70

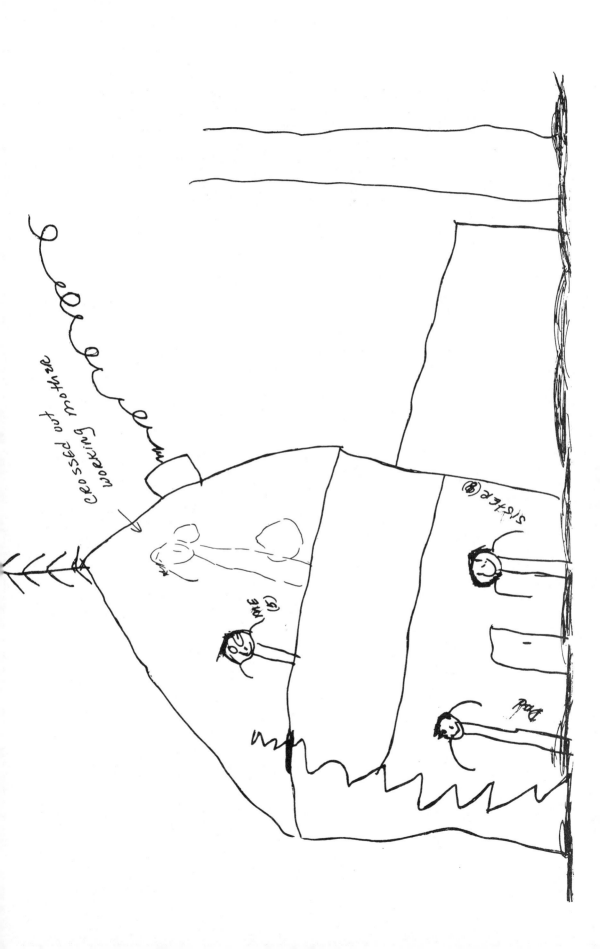

ALCOHOLIC PARENT – Drawing 71 by 13-year-old Bill reflects the devastating effects of alcoholism on the family. The father, with his bottle and his tormented face and isolation from the rest of the family, does not present a person with whom Bill can identify. Bill has no concept of himself in the family, as can be seen by the K-F-D-S. The extreme depression Bill feels, with a tormented mother crying and a brother fleeing into the world of books, is poignantly expressed in the K-F-D. The only face that is clear is that of the father. It is a dehumanized face. Father's addiction has devastated this family.

Dad
Drinking

Mom

Self
(13)

Brother (16)
Reading

DRAWING 71

BATTERING PARENT – In Drawing 72, we see a family in which the father has beaten the mother and the children frequently. Nine-year-old Greg seems to be trying to prevent the father from hitting the mother and perhaps protecting the little ones in the family. The father's face appears ominous. This little boy tries to identify with the father, who at times can be quite thoughtful. However, the degree of disturbance between the parents and the mother's passive acceptance of this man's brutality will make Greg's lot a difficult one in trying to identify with such a father. If Greg does identify with the father and marries, he may beat his family members.

DRAWING 72

Mom

Dad

Me
(9)

Little
Brother (8)
"crawling"

Big brother
(11)

Little
sister (3)

PSYCHOTIC PARENT – Seven-and-a-half-year old, John, who produced Drawing 73, has a father who has been diagnosed as a paranoid schizophrenic. The father is seen as a mechanical man. John
hides himself in the house next to his mother and he encapsulates
both of them for protection from the bizarre world of the father. Note
the lack of face on John.

DRAWING 73

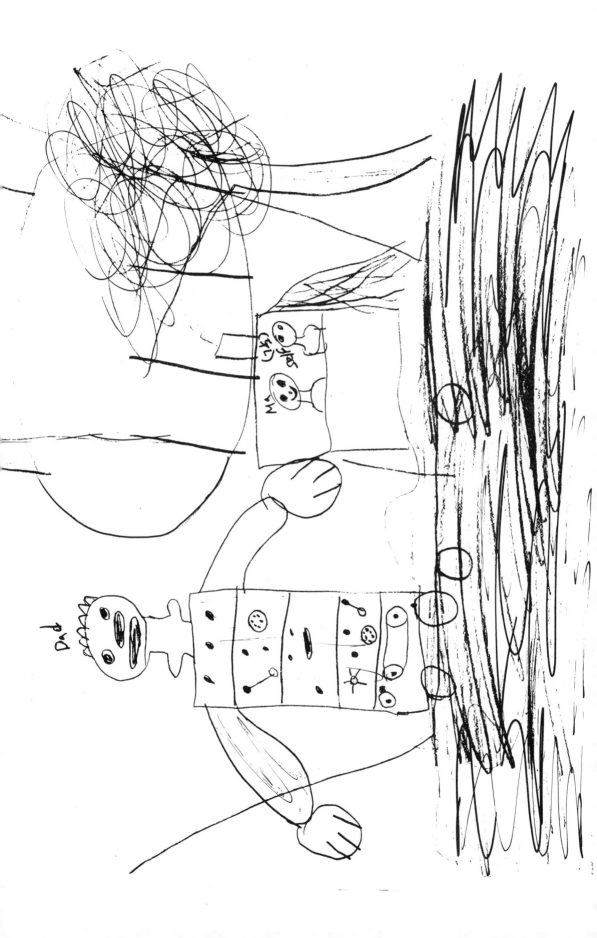

HOMOSEXUAL PARENT – For some children in our culture the problem of trying to identify with a homosexual parent in a nuclear family is, indeed, a difficult one.

Eleven-and-a-half-year-old Mike has a father who has homosexual problems which are known to the boy. The high-heeled father is seen in a very sketchy way in Drawing 74. There are peculiar distortions of the eyes. The boy is belittled by his father, as well as by the father's problems. Mike has great feelings of inferiority and feels like a clown. He acts like a clown in real life by trying to make other people laugh at him rather than with him. The mother, at the top of the page, appears angry – she is pointing a gun at the father. Mike finds no real identification in the family; rather, he plays the role of the fool. He is made to feel like a fool in this family because of the problems of identification with a father whose own identity is confused.

DRAWING 74

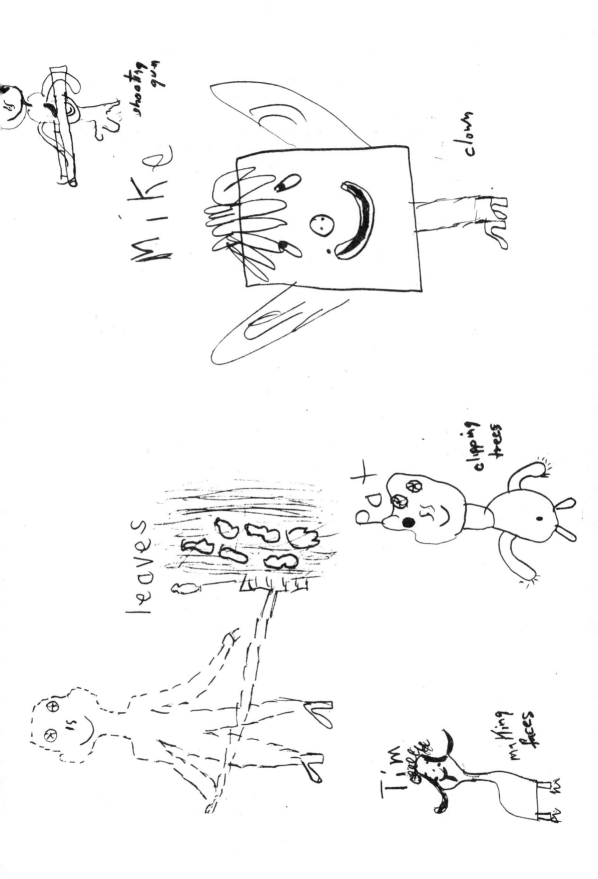

MISSING PARENT IDEALIZED – In Drawing 75 by 9-year-old Ed, we see a fantasized identification. Ed's father is in prison. We note the picture on the wall with the intense light beaming on the whole family and on the father. This little boy dreams about a father he cannot reach. He is still trying to identify with him, but identification with a picture must be quite unrewarding and incomplete.

DRAWING 75

IDENTIFICATION WITH OBJECTS RATHER THAN PEOPLE –
Sometimes, if identification with a parent is not possible, a child may identify with an object such as a gun, car, or motorcycle as a source of power.

In Drawing 76 made by 14-year-old George, we see the family without George in it. His father was very busy with activities outside the home, including hunting. He was a very frightened person but one who was very belligerent and aggressive. The symbols of the gun and knife which he carried were related to George's aggressive feelings about his father.

George refused to put himself in the family. Instead, he drew himself in Drawing 77 with his huge motorcycle. He tended to identify with the machine as a source of power. Shortly after leaving school, he "ran" with a motorcycle gang and his identification was with this anti-hero-oriented group. Thus, he sought power through identification with the motorcycle people rather than a distant father, closer to his gun and knife than his son.

Dad

Mom
COOKING

Kathy (12)
DOING DISHES

DRAWING 76

DRAWING 77

George (14)

Anne (9)

taking sister for
a motorbike ride

RUNAWAYS – Twelve-year-old Jerry, who produced Drawing 78, feels isolated in the present family structure. The mother has remarried and is felt to be close to the stepfather. We note that they are encapsulated and seen as close to each other but very distant from Jerry. There are other problems in the home, including a grandmother who has been ill and living with the family. These **add** to Jerry's feelings of being left out. He is moving off the page **and** apparently out of the family. Jerry has no roots or feet – only wheels to "move on." He has given up trying to find identity in a broken home and has become a rolling stone. He ran away shortly after producing K-F-D 78.

DRAWING 78

CHAPTER 7

LACK OF SELF-GROWTH: THE DEPRESSED AND SUICIDAL CHILD

When warmth and identification in the nuclear family or outside are not possible, feelings of isolation, coldness, and loneliness often begin which may lead to suicide.

The lack of identification is reflected in the numerous K-F-Ds with no faces, drawn by those who do not "see" themselves or others clearly and have no self-identity, as shown in Drawings 79, 80, and 81.

I. NO FACES

DRAWING 79

DRAWING 80

sister
9

Little
Sister

Dad

Going Away

mother

Sel

DRAWING 81

II. SEEKING EXCITEMENT AND WARMTH

In Drawing 82, we see that 16-year-old Laura refuses to include herself in the family. Instead she places her K-F-D-S on the other side of the paper, as shown in Drawing 82A.

She depicts herself in her room playing records and creating her own excitement through music and fantasy. Some fantasy is sexual as suggested by the vaginal-like record placement. Laura is psychologically moving away from the family into her own world.

Sister eating

Dad reading

Mom - Stringing String beans

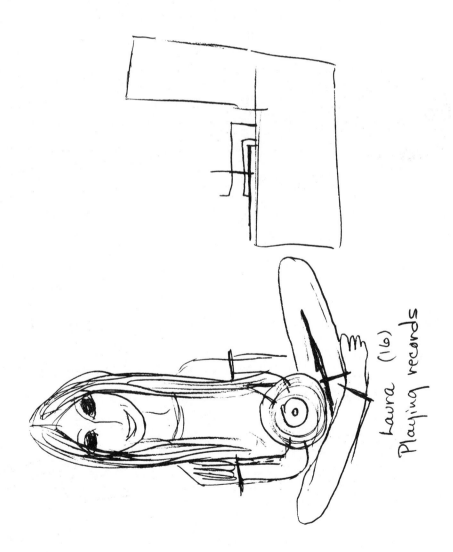

laura (16)
Playing records

Sometimes, when the world is unpredictable and lonely, a child will frantically create excitement – often of a sexual nature. Nine-year-old Marilyn's sexual preoccupations are vividly demonstrated in Drawing 83.

Marilyn has been in six foster homes. She tends to be very seductive and this has been one of the reasons for her removal from other homes. In Drawing 83, we see her sexual preoccupations very clearly and some of the related symbols. We note that the penis areas of the males in the drawing are emphasized and shaded, reflecting this little girl's obsessional preoccupation with sex. The open book on the table next to her seems to be displacement of her female genitalia. We note that the table covers this area in her own body. This type of denial and displacement of sexual symbol to the book are common in our K-F-Ds.

Marilyn had actually had intercourse with the 17-year-old foster brother. We note the darts (penis symbol) he is throwing and the target (vagina symbol) at which he is throwing them. The brothers standing in the bottom right-hand corner of the drawing have their pool cues, and the phallic implications of the cues with balls on the table are all related to Marilyn's great obsessional thoughts concerning sex. Marilyn seems to relate sex to love and is swept up by her sexual obsessions. She fights depression and coldness by continually seeking warmth.

DRAWING 83

setting table
Mother

Pool

Mike-15½   16½

Father

fixing tv

doll   14½

building model
brother-12½

shooting darts
brother 17½

reading   12

doing math
Me—9

Paul-11¼

III. MOON CHILDREN: DEPRESSION AND SUICIDE

In our previous book (14), we discussed the symbol of snow and coldness as associated with depression and suicide. Another common K-F-D symbol frequently associated with depression is the moon.

Traditionally, the sun has been viewed as the source of light and heat and consequently of life; hence, it has been regarded as a deity and worshipped as such by all primitive peoples, and has a leading place in all mythologies. *Ra* of the Egyptians, *Helos* of the Greeks, *Sol* of the Romans are only a few of the sun gods so worshipped. The sun is almost invariably feminine. The moon is almost always masculine to the Slavs, Hindus, Mexicans, etc. To this day the Germans have Frau Sonne (Mrs. Sun) and Herr Mond (Mr. Moon).

The moon has traditionally been a symbol containing things wanted but not present on earth, i.e., unanswered prayers, fruitless love, broken vows, etc. To cry for the moon has meant to crave for what is really beyond one's reach on earth. A lunatic is one who is moonstruck. Nothing grows in the "black light" of the cold moon. There is a high frequency of morbid moon fascination in children with unrequited love for a parent, usually the father.

Consider the D-A-P made by 16-year-old Heidi – a wondrous portrayal of a tearful moon-maiden. Heidi had bouts of severe depression and repetitive suicide thoughts. Heidi's K-F-D is seen in Drawing 85. See the K-F-D-S turned away from view but next to the boxed, intense father. Heidi is preoccupied with the underwater fish world, a water obsession found in many depressive people. Heidi tried valiantly to get close to the intellectualizing, perfectionistic father but never succeeded by her standards.

DRAWING 84

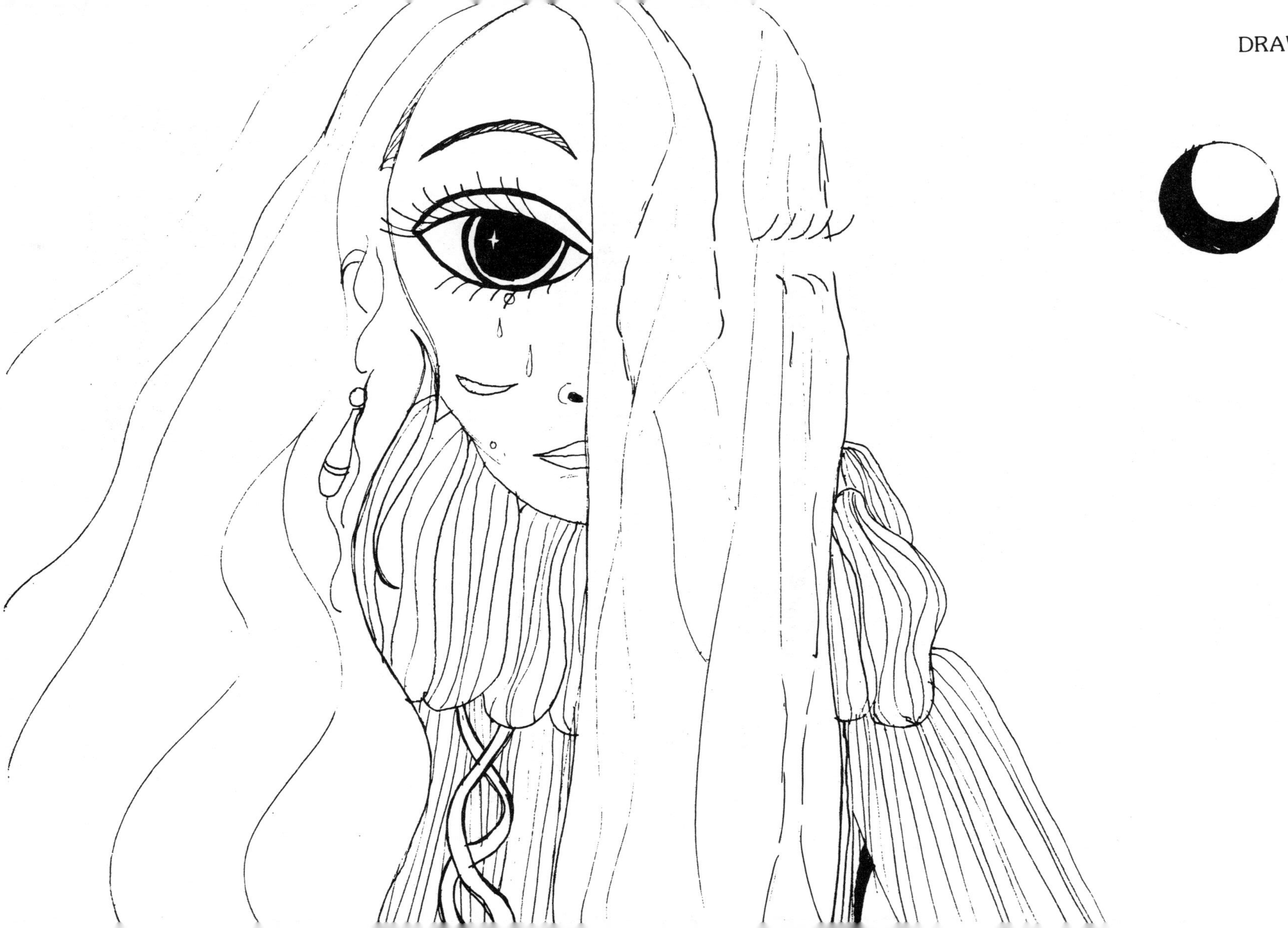

DRAWING 85

The recurrent theme of moon drawings related to difficulty in identification and acceptance by the father is seen in Drawing 86 by 14-year-old Gerald.

Gerald had been rejected by his father throughout his life and had just returned from foster home placement to live with the father. The dad has his back turned and the moonlight beams through the rain from dad's direction. Gerald remained depressed and self-destructive living with the recently remarried father. It was eventually necessary to remove him from the destructive dad and place Gerald with the mother, who had also remarried.

One week after K-F-D 86, Gerald produced K-F-D 87 depicting his family living with the mother.

The moon is in the compartment with the stepdad; the style stays the same. However, the K-F-D-S has regressed and appears much younger than in K-F-D 86. Some subtle changes have occurred to the K-F-D-S in 87. The self is now ascendent and facing the stepfather. The moon is now in the stepdad's compartment rather than in Gerald's, and is much smaller. The rain has stopped falling on Gerald; he is less depressed and suicidal than he was when living with the dad. Dads, however, are still associated with moonlight rather than sunlight.

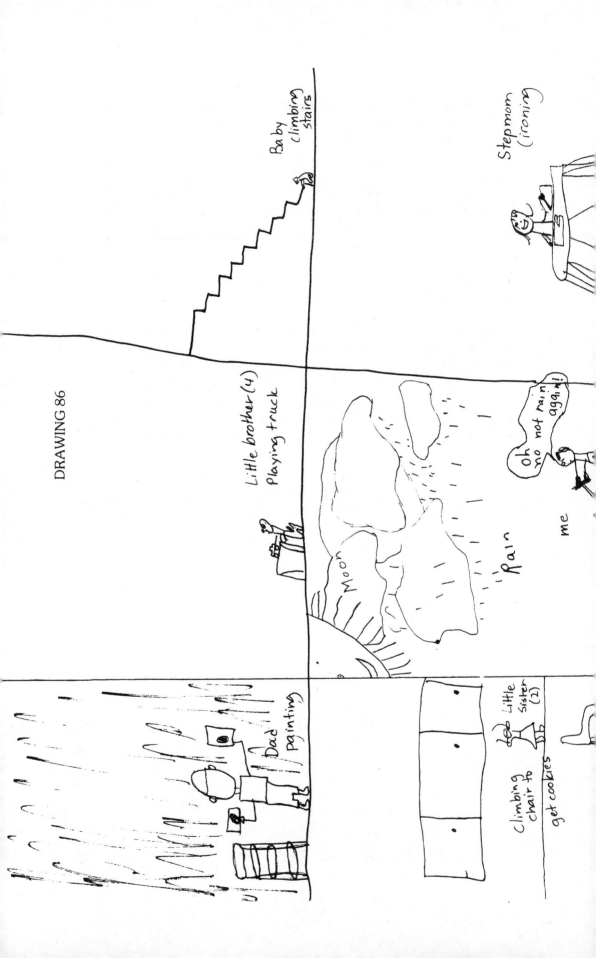

DRAWING 86

DRAWING 87

The glum moon shines on 11-year-old Maria's Dad, "walking in the moonlight," as seen in K-F-D 88. The tiny helpless-appearing precariously balanced K-F-D-S is trying to get to the nurturing yet aggressive mother, but must chance passing the ferocious-appearing brother. The dad is transfixed, as if on a cross, and his moonlight mood is transmitted to his daughter, who had depressive bouts, as did the father.

DRAWING 88

Ten-year-old Donna drew K-F-D 89. "The moon" is in largest print and dominates the mood. Donna said of her K-F-D, "Everybody is watching TV. My room is on top. The police came in at night to see if my dad was there but he was gone. Prince, the dog, is barking because he doesn't know the police." The police have faces, the family members have none. Donna was removed from this home and placed in foster care. She had depressive bouts associated with her desire to be close to her faceless dad in the moonlight shadow.

DRAWING 89

In Drawing 90, Howard pathetically portrays his feelings as an outsider in this family, taking out the garbage in the moonshine. Howard often thinks of death, which reflects his depression; he seems to seek tragedy and moonshine in his life rather than happiness and sunshine.

DRAWING 90

IV. PARENTAL REJECTION – SUICIDE

In Drawing 91, by 21-year-old Gwen, a desperate attempt is reflected in her effort to identify with the mother. Gwen was a product of the mother's first marriage and the mother had extreme difficulty in relating to her. At times, there was significant rejection.

The mother had a 2-year-old child by her second marriage. Note how Gwen has shut herself off from the mother, both by the shell around the K-F-D-S and the wall between the mother and the rest of the family. The mother is huge in Gwen's thoughts, and if mother were complete, she would, of course, dominate the entire drawing.

Gwen has attempted suicide. She has desperately tried to get close to her mother. The mother has recently tried to get closer and be less rejecting. At the time the drawing was done, identification was being attempted, but she was obsessed with her inability to break through mother's shell.

Gwen's obsessive, desperate desire for closeness to her mother brings to mind the well-known study by A. Freud and D. Burlingham (32) of children separated from their families and living in residential nurseries during World War II. The authors mentioned that ". . . emotions that would normally be directed toward parents remain undeveloped and unsatisfied, but . . . latent in the child and ready to leap into action the moment the slightest opportunity for attachment is offered . . . " (p. 63).

DRAWING 91

Gwen's torment in her inability to get close to or identify with her mother is reflected in her D-A-P face shown in Drawing 92. This face reflects the torment leading to Gwen's suicide attempts. Inability to identify with a parent, and a continuing attempt to do so, can lead to lifelong anguish and depression.

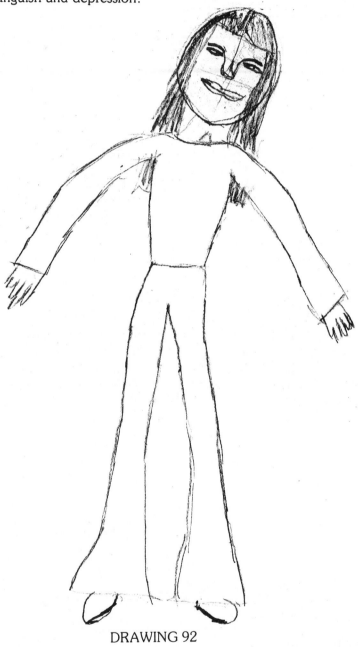

DRAWING 92

CHAPTER 8

LONGITUDINAL STUDIES IN SELF-DEVELOPMENT

I. DANIEL FROM AGES 3 TO 11:
A STRUGGLE FOR IDENTITY

Daniel's family lived several hundred miles from my office in an isolated area. They brought their son in for "checkups." Because of their isolation, they were never able to get help for Daniel, although it was suggested to them many times. However, they faithfully brought him in for his "checkup." Daniel has left us, through his K-F-Ds, a chronicle of his struggles and heartaches and failure to establish identity within his family.

189

In Drawing 93, we see Daniel's view of his family. It is possible for a bright 3-year-old to depict his family and their relative sizes and, thus, their importance to him.

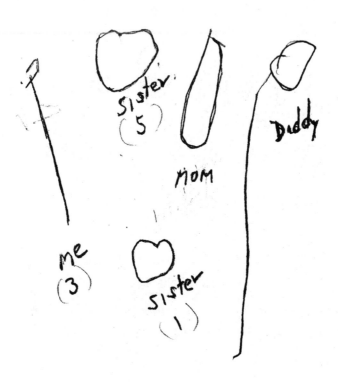

DRAWING 93

When Daniel was 5½, he produced Drawing 94. The family is close together. No figures are isolated. Dad remains quite large, but we note the K-F-D-S developing and the large hands on the Self, which were then erased, as if he is getting ready to feel his power but is careful at this time to conceal this urge.

DRAWING 94

When Daniel was 6, he produced Drawing 95. In this picture, we see Daniel at the top of the page, very close to his father but above him and, perhaps, dominating him. Aside from the long necks suggesting dependency, the drawing is relatively normal.

At age 7½, Daniel was seen and produced Drawing 96. At this time, Daniel was having symptoms of soiling himself. We note the sister, three-and-a-half years younger, with a repetition of a figure inside of her. This is said to be a doll, but as it turned out, it also appears to be Daniel's "alter ego" or "other Self." He acted much younger than his sister. The total stress within this family started to affect Daniel and caused him to regress.

191

DRAWING 95

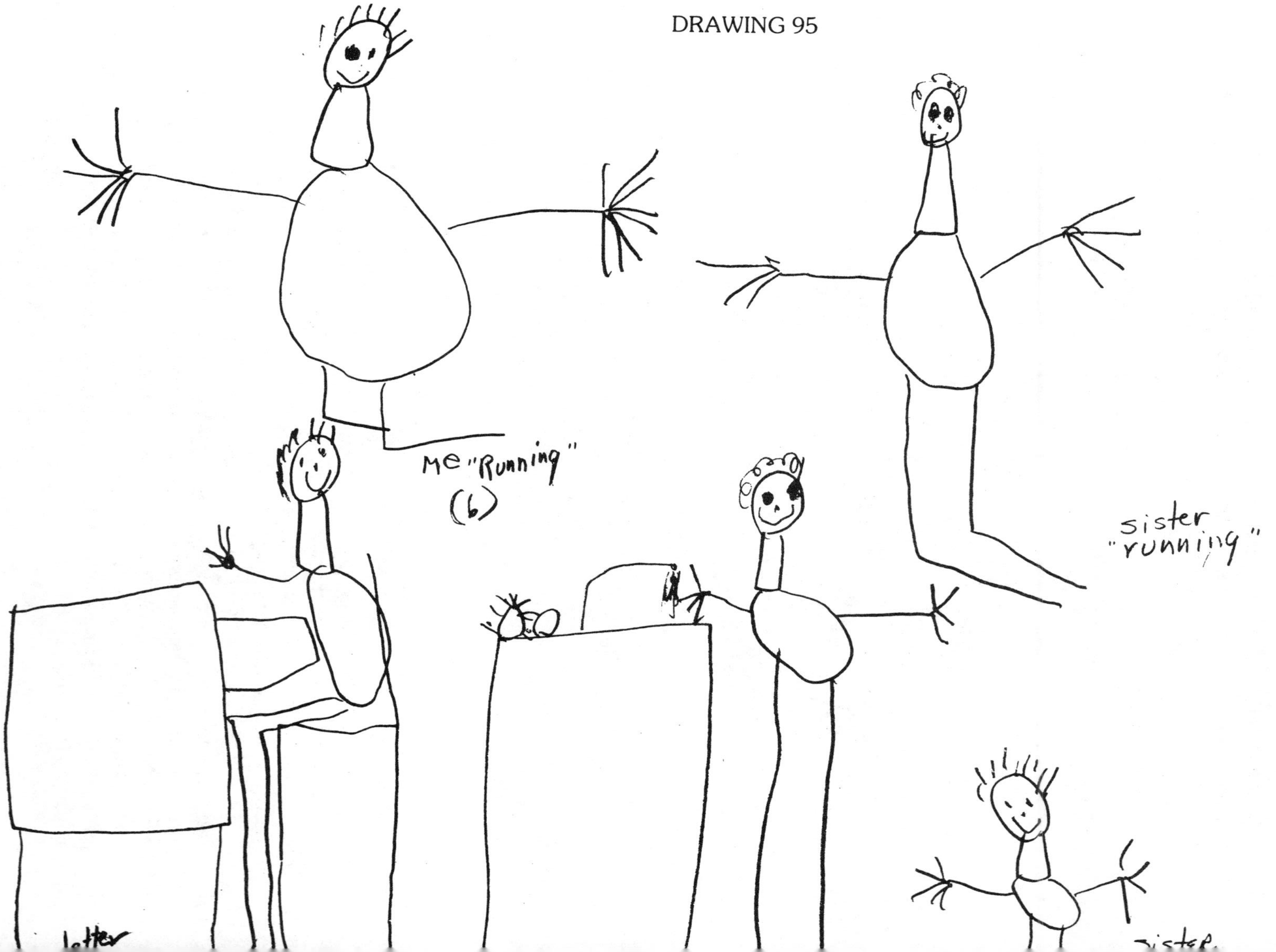

sister "running"

sister

Me "Running"
(6)

latter

DRAWING 96

mom

Dad

sister
(4)

(9)
sister

self
7½

When Daniel was 8, he produced Drawing 97. We note again the repetition of the figure within the younger sister. Daniel continues to feel inferior and is in the lower right-hand corner of the drawing. The heavy shading of the figure within the sister suggests Daniel's anxiety about his identification with her and his distance from dad. Daniel's soiling and other regressive behavior continued.

DRAWING 97

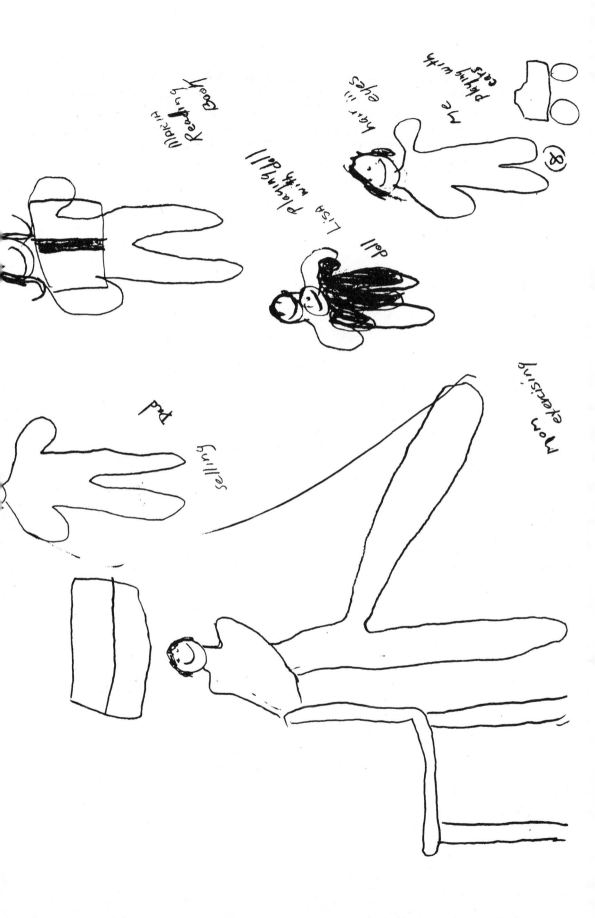

At 8½, Daniel did Drawing 98. He no longer soils himself. In order to "get attention" (to get enough love to identify and grow?), Daniel now dramatizes small hurts. He has a downcast mouth and wears a cast. For the first time, both sisters are doubled and Daniel has two "other selves." He is making heroic but pathetic attempts to "get attention."

DRAWING 98

When Daniel was 9, he made Drawing 99. For the first time, the K-F-D-S is in a box, as are the other family members. The father is pleading with the mother (indeed, the parents were having increased marital problems). Daniel's shaking of the tree with the leaves (dependency symbols) falling suggests his anger at not having his dependency needs met. If we look carefully, we can be see that the eye of the K-F-D-S is turned toward the parents. Daniel was described by the parents as being "bad and annoying" and "doing all sorts of things to get attention." The K-F-D sisters are both doubled and Daniel was described as a "sissy" and "girlish."

DRAWING 99

At 9½, Daniel completed Drawing 100. The family members are still compartmentalized. Daniel is beating (casting out?) his older sister. The mother is faceless and legless. Mother was threatening to leave the family. She is viewed as having no feet (no roots?). The younger sister is faceless and appears helpless. Father has dependency needs of his own which are threatened by the possible departure of his wife. Daniel is angry and acts out more at home. He is playing soccer and is described as less "girlish." The sisters are no longer doubled. Daniel no longer seeks his identity in his sister.

DRAWING 100

In Drawing 101 done at the age of 10, we see Daniel's attempt to get close to the father, but the father is bent over. Each family member is in his or her own box. Daniel looks angry and frustrated.

DRAWING 101

Drawing 102, done when Daniel was 10½, shows him moving out of the family. The parents were in the midst of a divorce. The father was depressed; the mother had regressed. Both of the older children were finding their identifications outside of the family. The youngest child was still demanding mother's attention. Daniel probably will continue throughout his life to search for his identification. He will feel a lack of completeness until he finds it. Because of the parental problems, the boy was unable to identify within the family, although he had tried valiantly. This last picture shows him taking off into the world – a "rolling stone" searching for a person or causes with whom or which he can identify.

The isolated living situation of Daniel and his family and the reluctance of his parents to enter counseling made therapeutic intervention impractical.

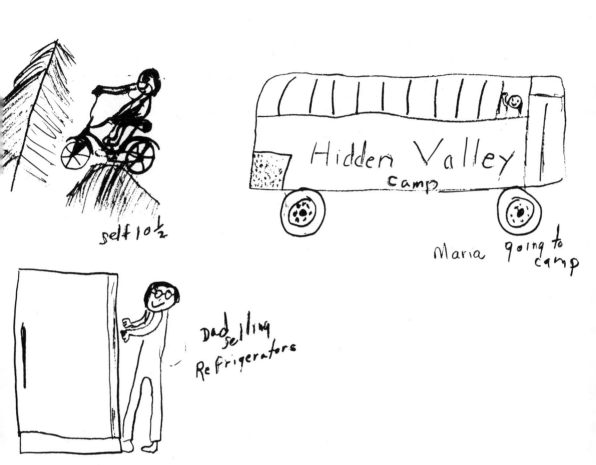

self 10½

Hidden Valley
camp

Maria going to camp

Dad selling Refrigerators

LisA

Mom
Reading
story

DRAWING 102

II. BILL FROM AGES 3 TO 11: THE OUTSIDER

Bill made K-F-D 103 when he was 3½. Subsequently, the parents were divorced and the two sons lived with the father.

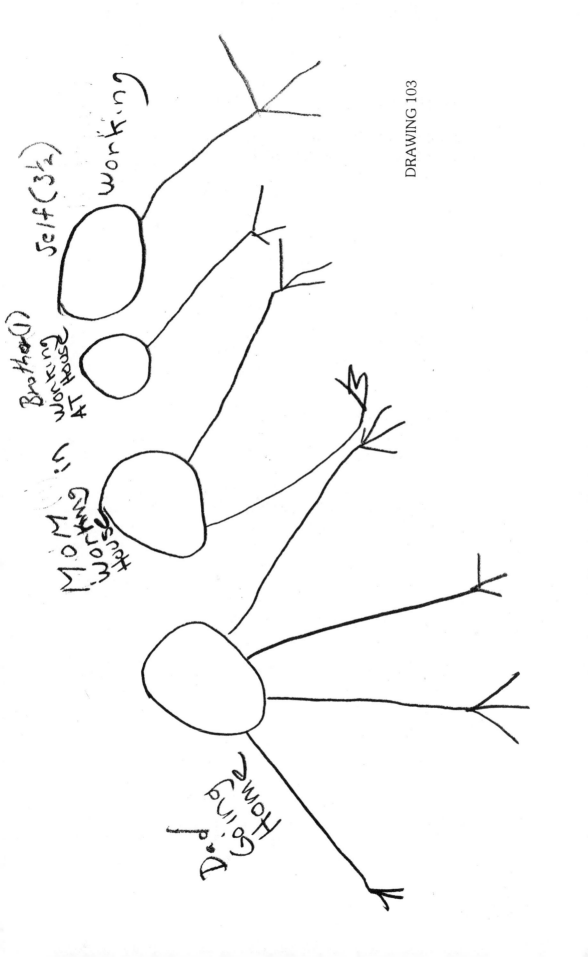

Self (3½)
working

Brother (1)
working
AT HOUSE

MoM
working

Dad
Home

DRAWING 103

When the mother remarried, Bill came to live with her at age 8 and drew K-F-D 104.

We see Bill doubling himself in a desperate effort to be somebody. The stepfather was extremely immature and could not accept Bill, intervening between Bill and his mother.

DRAWING 104

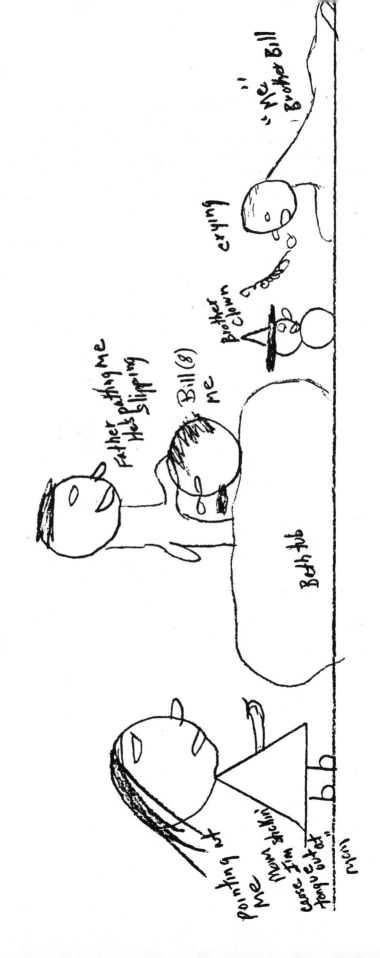

"Me"
Brother Bill

crying

Brother
Clown

Father bathing me
He's slipping

Bill (8)
me

Bath Tub

pointing at
Me
Mom sticking
tonge Im
case I'm
tongue out at"

When Bill was 9 he produced Drawing 105, in which we see a full-face K-F-D, as if Bill is asking for attention. We note the large, controlling arms. Bill was acting out and attracting everyone's attention. The mother and stepfather had a son but were divorced. The mother then remarried the second husband, and in Drawing 106, when Bill was 10, he drew his view of the family. As can be seen, the other three members of the family were fairly close together, but Bill is the outsider.

Mom
cooking dinner

Bill (9)
"jumping over a fence"

Brother (1½)
watching tv

DRAWING 106

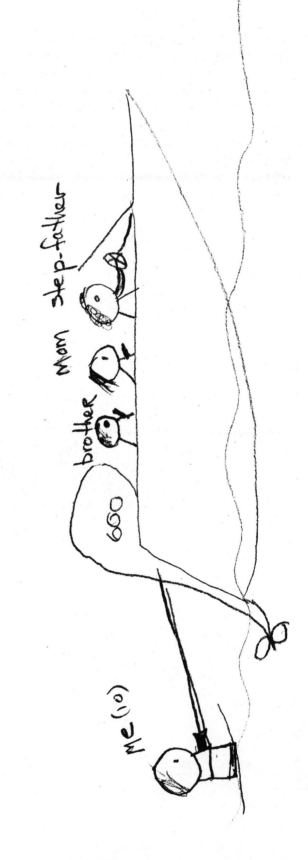

When Bill was 11, he produced Drawing 107. We note the faceless family members, including Bill, who seems to be swimming but perhaps sinking. Bill had always tried to relate to father figures but was unable to do so. He has very poor self-control at the present time. He has very little self and perhaps the family will be fragmented again by divorce. Bill has developed over the years into a faceless person, who does not know himself. Thus, he has none of the hyphenated words that go with self, such as self-control and self-esteem. Faceless selves are prone to be easily influenced and to imitate others such as dictators or religious fanatics. They have no identity and so easily and chameleon-like adopt the attitudes and behavior of others.

DRAWING 107

III. DIANE FROM AGES 5 TO 7: WITHDRAWAL

Five-year-old Diane produced Drawing 108. The parents were divorced and Diane was living with her father, brother, and grandmother. The drawing shows a closeness to the father and total family unity with everyone holding hands.

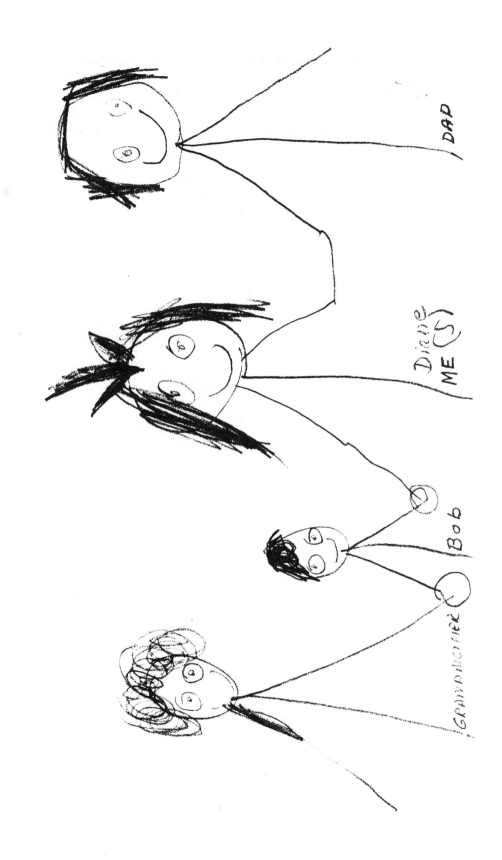

In Drawing 109, done when Diane was 5½, we note the change of expression from her first drawing. The father's happy expression has gone. The little girl is no longer holding hands with her father but with her brother. The expressions are much more worried and express much less happiness than those in the initial drawing. Diane's K-F-D-S has become smaller. The moon has entered the picture.

DRAWING 109

Diane

Bob

Dad

Grandma

The father had continuing problems with a depressive reaction to his divorce. In Drawing 110, done when Diane was 6, we see the little girl's concern for her father with the long-armed policeman berating the father. Note the smallness of the K-F-D-S and, particularly, of the little brother under the pressure of family stress related to the father's inability to control his moods.

DRAWING 110

Hat

POLICE OFFICER

GO TO JAIL

In Daddy's lap but police officers said I wasn't supposed to BE

Playing Cops and robbers
Bob

ME

Dad throwing oranges at Police officer

Dad- Driving too fast

CAT

When Diane was 6½, she produced Drawing 111. We see the beginning of compartmentalization. She is unwilling to complete the figures and each one is isolated, regressed, and expressionless. Diane has completed the process of withdrawing into her box and has made a turtle adjustment to life. Box people have few, if any friends, are narcissistic and "don't really care" about the world around them unless life in the box is threatened.

DRAWING 111

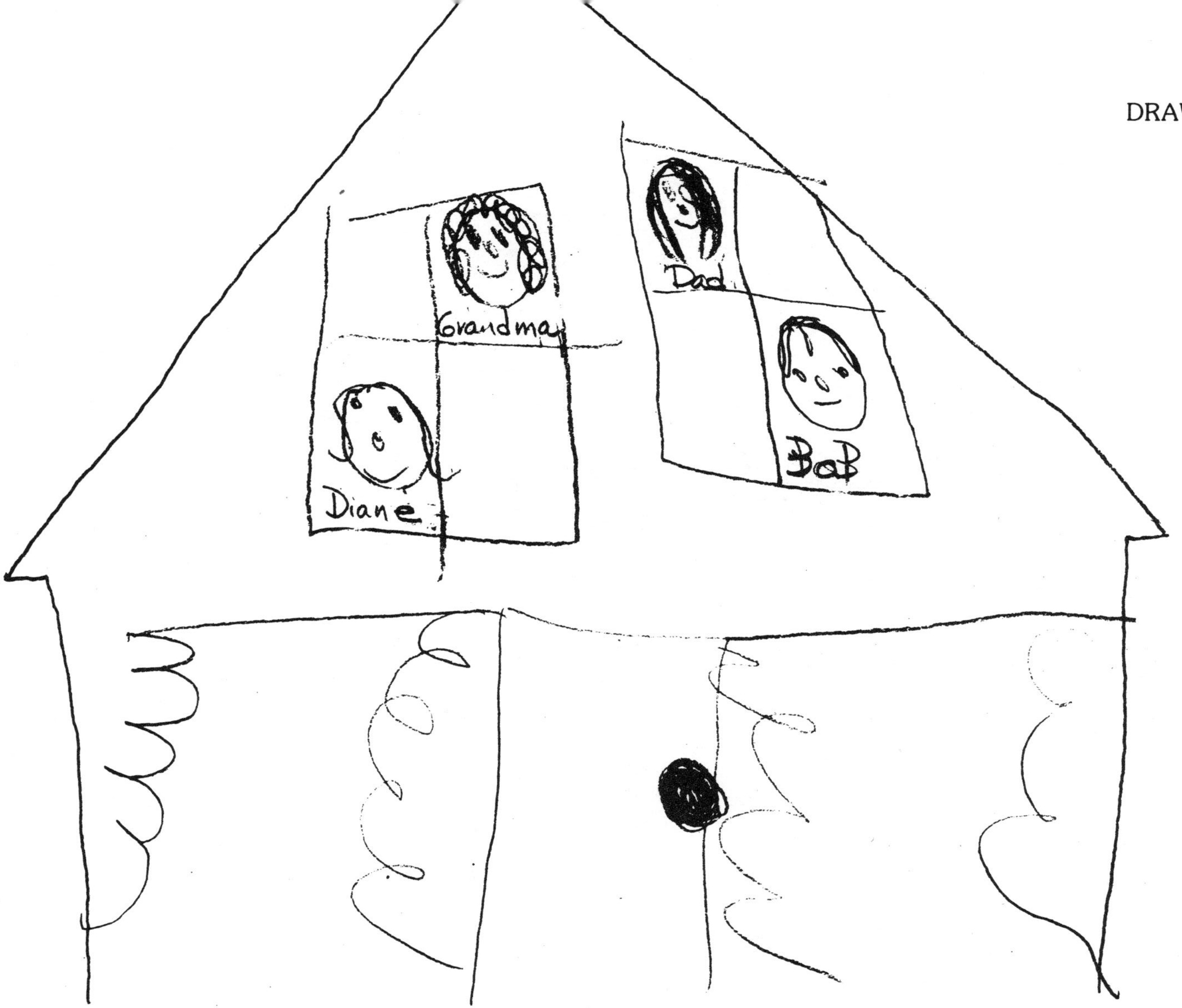

In K-F-D 112, completed when Diane was 6¾, we see the completion of her withdrawal from family. What appeared to be a happy 5-year-old girl turned into a very unhappy 7-year-old. Diane had reacted to the parents' divorce and the father's resulting depressive reaction by withdrawal.

For many children the need for early intervention and family counseling can be defined by the K-F-D. In addition, changes in the K-F-D Self help to measure counseling effectiveness.

DRAWING 112

CHAPTER 9

K-F-D USE IN SELF-GROWTH: CHILD ABUSE, FOSTER AND ADOPTIVE HOME PLACEMENT, FAMILY THERAPY

The K-F-D can be used effectively to improve understanding of family dynamics and as a therapeutic aid in counseling. It can be used in documenting progress in therapy as well as a tool to evaluate optimal foster and adoptive home placement.

I. K-F-D USE IN CHILD ABUSE

The K-F-D can be used in understanding and helping families in which there is child abuse.

Eight-year-old Kirk's K-F-D portrays more vividly than words a home with a battering father. The style is folded compartments (FOLCOM) associated with acute severe stress. In K-F-D 113 the fold is done so intensely that the paper is ripped on the fold and barely hanging together, reflecting Kirk's need to be separated from this brutality. This K-F-D was instrumental in getting intervention and help for this family.

At the Wayne County Juvenile Courts' Clinic for Child Study in Detroit, Michigan, the K-F-D has been used for ten years. Consulting psychiatrist H.M. Schornstein and his co-worker, J. Derr, have reported extensively on the practical use of the K-F-D in clinical settings. The following are some quotes from their article in the Interna-

DRAWING 113

tional Journal of Child Abuse (67) which may be of help to those working in similar clinical settings.

Since 1970, K-F-Ds have been routinely obtained at our Clinic for Child Study. Parents are given a blank paper and standard K-F-D instructions are given.

K-F-Ds are a non-verbal task, and clients may be more at ease with it. As one cannot cheat or lie, data are more meaningful.

We have found the K-F-Ds to be helpful in engaging parents. They are nearly always curious, and when asked questions about their own drawings, they generally become quite productive. Some spontaneously interpret their own or their spouse's drawings. Parents can often understand visually an aspect of their family relationship when they have not been able to comprehend it verbally. Discussion of the K-F-Ds with parents offers an additional dimension to both evaluative and treatment sessions.

K-F-Ds can be used to access impulse control, judgment, where responsibility is perceived to repose (not infrequently with the child), reality testing, interpersonal skills, and degree of organization. We have discovered siblings who were in danger. K-F-Ds have shown who perpetrated the abuse when responsibility has been unclear, unknown, or denied.

The parents have been asked to draw their family with themselves included. Which family do they consider as their family? Is the family complete? Is it the nuclear past family or the present family? It is important to note omissions – particularly if the impaired child or drawer is absent. Are other figures outside of the immediate family included in the drawing? This is important in assessing the client's ability to identify a family of his own.

The content of the drawings can depict developmental areas that are posing difficulties for the parents in their childrearing.

We have seen the child drawn as a competitor – for example, fathers who draw their sons as being more masculine, aggressive, or larger than themselves, or as being with the mother. Child abuse can develop in these instances when the parent regards the child as receiving more attention than the spouse – or an extension of the spouse.

Protective Services workers utilize the drawings as means of putting clients at ease via a non-verbal task and developing a better understanding of the people with whom they are working, and for enchancing their clinical judgment. When doubt exists as to whether to file an abuse/neglect petition with the Juvenile

Court, the K-F-D becomes a rapid and objective means until a full evaluation is available (pp. 1-5).

Schornstein and Derr summarize some benefits in clinical practice of K-F-D use:

1) Assessing individual and family psychodynamics and evolving a practical treatment plan.
2) Engaging clients and workers.
3) Rapidly obtaining projective corroborative data during the time charts are active.
4) Determining the effectiveness of therapy.
5) Assisting the timing of the return of abused children.
6) Alerting the staff to areas of potential family stresses.
7) Indicating the need for continued family supervision.
8) Verifying the reliability of new workers who might present a distorted clinical picture for consultations.

K-F-Ds may be useful not only in child abuse, but also in a variety of counseling or family-oriented services.

II. COUNSELING AND FOSTER HOME PLACEMENT FOR SALLY

Sally had been in a house where the mother had been shot and killed by the father. She was removed to a foster home, and when first seen at age 7, produced Drawing 114. Even with a great deal of time and urging, Sally was unable to produce any more.

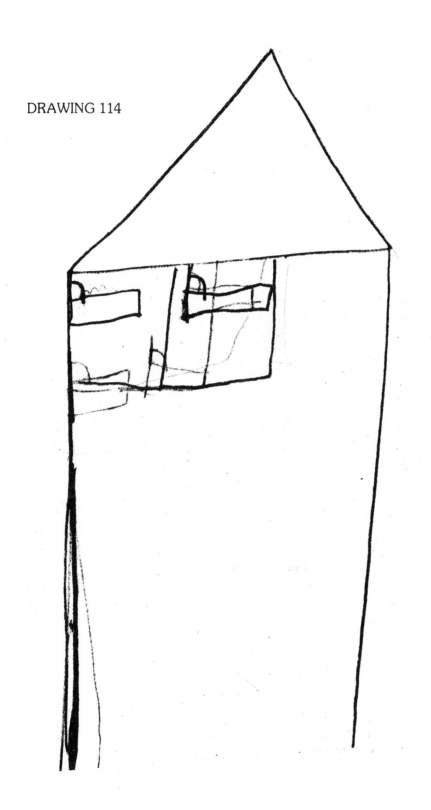

DRAWING 114

After six months in the foster home, Sally was seen for reevaluation, when she did Drawing 115. We see the crosshatching at the top of the drawing reflecting her obsessive-compulsive defenses. She did make bedrooms for the people, actually placing their names in them, but the people are missing.

DRAWING 115

When Sally was 8 years old, the K-F-D was repeated and she produced Drawing 116. The foster "mom" is ascendent in the family. We see Sally in a compartment with the 12-year-old foster brother, Joe, who was her protector. Sally was able to produce figures in the family and although they were still encapsulated she does show the emergence of her Self through the drawings.

At the time the last K-F-D was made, she was progressing normally in school. She was still apprehensive and very much needed the safety of adults or older brothers, but Sally was growing and gaining in self-confidence.

Ray (9)

Tres
Inside
Tree

Joann

John

MOM
(30)

me
(8)

Joe
(12)

III. EVALUATION OF THERAPY: SCOTT, A
CASE OF SEVERE ANXIETY REACTION

Scott was referred for counseling because of severe anxieties; his first K-F-D production is seen in Drawing 117.

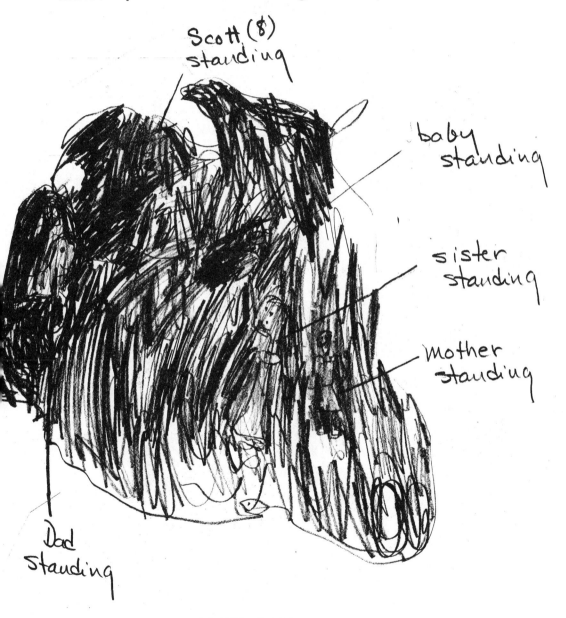

DRAWING 117

There are some figures hidden in Drawing 117, but they are extremely difficult to see because of the scribbling, a clinical indicator of anxiety.

Scott was seen in treatment and one month later produced K-F-D 118. The figures in this drawing are again vague and partial; they are difficult to discriminate. However, there is much less shading (anxiety) and the figures are emerging.

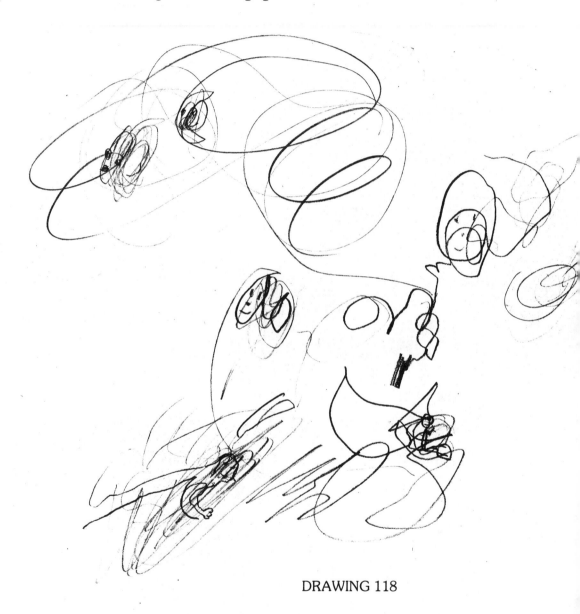

DRAWING 118

In Scott's Drawing 119, done one month later, we see the intensity of the shading diminshed. The dynamics in the family contributing to Scott's severe anxiety are more clearly shown.

We view the encapsulated figure of the 10-year-old retarded sister. In this family, the sister preoccupied the mother and Scott felt rejected by the mother. We see the similarity in the heads of Scott and his sister. Scott had extreme ambivalence toward his sister in a family in which there were great pressures not to show anger toward this sister. This contributed to Scott's severe anxiety reaction. Scott was able to reduce his anxiety. Both parents, particularly the mother, became involved and responded to therapy. The family reaction to the 10-year-old retarded sister, encapsulated repeatedly in Scott's K-F-D, became the focal point for therapy.

Drawing 119 reflects an emergence of the Self from severe anxiety. In Scott's drawings, we saw diffuse anxiety with very little defense.

DRAWING 119

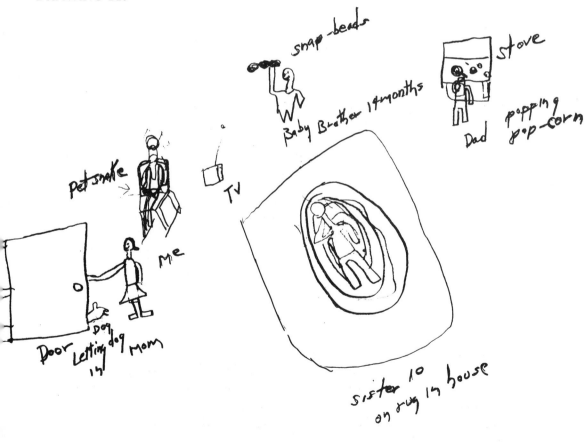

IV. EVALUATION OF COUNSELING:
   THE CASE OF DAVID

David, an exceptionally bright boy, did not defend himself with
massive anxiety as did Scott. Instead, he tended to regress and express himelf in bodily symptoms. David produced Drawing 120 when
he was 6¾-years-old. The face is rather grim, but the drawing, with
the exception of a long neck, appears "normal."

DRAWING 120

On the same day, David produced Drawing 121. He had been
referred because of soiling problems, as well as extreme passive-
aggressive behavior. Note the central theme of the vicious dog encapsulated with David and his 5-year-old sister. The parents were
"upstairs." Drawing 121 reflects David's obsessive thoughts related to
anger and his sister.

DRAWING 121

After three months of therapy, David produced Drawing 122. The sister now has a face and "the dog bit her." The parents now have faces and are not encapsulated. David is central and urging the dog to bite. The dog is having a bowel movement near the father's head. David's K-F-D-S has come from his shell. In Drawing 122, there are no barriers or boxes. David has emerged from his box in Drawing 121 to become a strong, "open" person. His neurotic symptoms and defenses are alleviated and the parents can reason with and enjoy this strong-willed young man.

In David's case, as with most children, it is much more meaningful to work with the whole family or at least include the parents, rather than working with an isolated child.

DRAWING 122

Dog
Charch!
Mev
David
Malking dog rambunctious so it will bite
"shit"
Sob Sob!
Sister
5
Dog bit her
yipy!
Dog
father
yahoo!
at Dog
mother

V. FAMILY THERAPY: K-F-D IN COLOR –
THE THREE SISTERS

A mother was very concerned about her three daughters and wanted to understand them. The daughters – Sally, 8, Jill, 13, and Cathy, 17 – produced K-F-Ds used as a basis for some family therapy sessions.

A. *Sister #1: Sally, Age 8 – The Baby*

Sally, age 8, produced K-F-D 123. She places herself at the bottom of the drawing, facing mom. Dad is outside the family riding his bike. The older ascendent sister, Cathy, is drawn as large and domineering. Cathy's face is black, while all other family members have various colored facial characteristics. Cathy, with her long yellow hair, is drawn furthest from the parents. Jill, the serious student, is central and seen as the hub of the family. Mom is halved and drawn among her flowers and in a subordinate position. Sally has tiny arms and extended feet (skis) and looks at mother for guidance. Red is often called the child's color (Santa Claus, baby toys, etc.) and appears to be Sally's favorite color for her K-F-D-S.

DRAWING 123

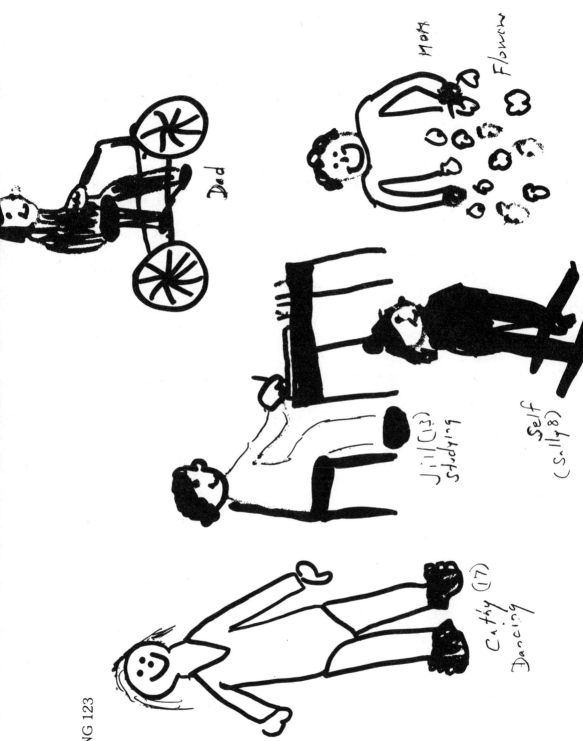

Dad

Mom

Flower

Jill (13)
Studying

Self
(Sally 8)

Cathy (17)
Dancing

B. Sister #2: Jill, Age 13 – The Outgoing, Competitive Sister

Jill, viewed by Sally as the hub of the family, is described by the parents as assertive but the most open and communicative of the sisters. In her K-F-D 124 Jill colors herself red, as does Sally. Highly competitive Jill is playing both tennis and soccer, reflecting her vigorous, outwardly directed competition. Jill is a "doer." The ball as a K-F-D symbol is used most frequently by competitive children directing their energies (depicted by the ball) outward.

She depicts Sally as subordinate and protected by mother. The parents as well as big sister Cathy are ascendent and "looked up to" by Jill. Jill appears to be willing to "play ball with" and "respect" authority figures. Mother is the "hub" of Jill's K-F-D world. Dad is the most distant family member, present but rather drab appearing with "X's" on Jill's tennis racket (an arm extension). The "X's" reflect Jill's controls; she is competitive but has a strong conscience and tries to control her aggressiveness.

Ascendent Cathy is viewed as a "painted doll," showing off her long hair, painted face, and long legs. Jill views the family clearly and realistically. Cathy is colored blue, a colder color than emotional red.

Soccer Ball

Self
Jill (13)

Cathy (17)
Dancing

Mom

Tennis
Ball

Sally (8)

Dad

C. Sister #3: Cathy, Age 17 – The Introverted, Competitive Sister

Cathy refused to place herself in her K-F-D 125. The cold blue color permeates the entire drawing and reflects Cathy's blue mood. Sally depicted Cathy's black emotionless face in K-F-D 123. Jill drew Cathy blue in K-F-D 124.

The broad-shouldered dad dominates K-F-D 125. This is a view of dad not shared by the other sisters in their K-F-Ds. The parents are viewed as dominant. Little sister Sally is seen as "inferior" and at a level with the dog. Jill is seen as very close to the mother, studying and seeking the mother's attention. Thus each sister views the next youngest sister as closest to the mother, with the youngest sister also depicting herself closest to mom.

What about the scribbling below the mother's waist (table)? While dad is depicted as a complete, powerful person, mother is "halved" and not seen from the waist down, nor are the sisters drawn clearly below the waist. From Jill's picture we see painted-faced, "leggy" Cathy trying hard to be "feminine." This was verified by the parents. For example, Cathy reportedly spent "hours putting on her face," and refused to be seen in public without her "face on."

Cathy appears to have identified with the perceived power of the father in the family and has a clouded, distorted, incomplete, "halved" version of the mother. Cathy's struggle to find a harmonious self-identification at this stage of her life has resulted in a "blue mood" of denial and depression and increasing narcissism.

Through family sessions the parents and three sisters are able to better understand the family dynamics. The parents in particular became increasingly aware of the needs and strivings so poignantly shown in the K-F-Ds of the three sisters.

DRAWING 125

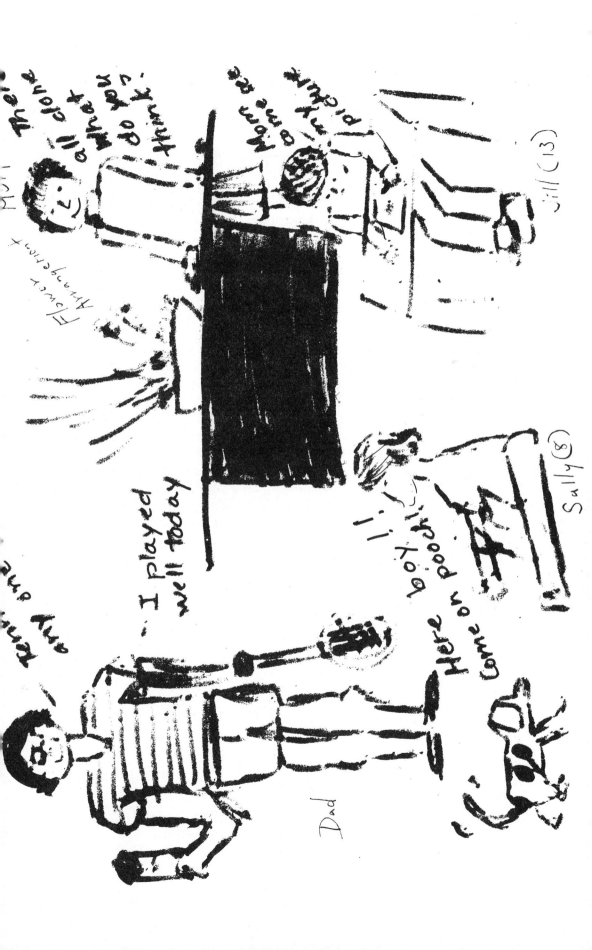

VI. FAMILY THERAPY: DEPENDENCE – PARENT AND CHILD K-F-Ds

Oftentimes, dependent people become angry when their dependency needs are not met, as reflected in K-F-Ds 126, 127 and 128 by the Green Family.

K-F-D 126 was done by mom Green. See how the arms of the dad and two sons are elongated, a carry-over from mom's childhood relations to a frightening dad. In reality her husband and sons were not punishing.

Buttons in human figure drawings have been clinically associated with dependency (14, 53). In K-F-D 126 mom places buttons on the dad and eldest son, suggesting that she looks to them as a source of nurturance, which indeed she did.

DRAWING 126

Younger Son

Older Son

Mom

Dad

K-F-D 127 by the eldest son, Charlie, shows the mom with buttons. In this child-dominated home (children on top of drawing), Charlie still looked to the mom for nurturing.

SELF (12)

Brother (10)

MOM

Dad

K-F-D 128 was drawn by dad Green. Dad places buttons on mom and seems to be wistfully looking up in hope of being nurtured. When this family is together, dad looks to mom for nurturance; the oldest son looks to mom for nurturance; and mom looks to dad and the oldest son for nurturance. Jealousy and childishness dominated family relations until these dynamics were uncovered, understood, and corrected. Drawings 126, 127 and 128 attempt to demonstrate that buttons as K-F-D symbols are placed on figures toward whom dependency needs are directed.

DRAWING 128

Mom   older son   younger son

KWASAKI

Dad

VII. DEPENDENCY ON AN ALCOHOLIC FATHER

In K-F-D 129, the 13-year-old drawer places buttons on dad and thus looks to him for nurturance. Tormented, drinking dad seems incapable of meeting his son's needs. Yet the son looks to dad for help and nurturing and appears to want to be in dad's world. If the son joins or is attracted to dad's world, a world of torment but perceived nourishment, the son, too, may well become an alcoholic.

During family therapy the father, after seeing his son's K-F-D, was shocked into joining Alcoholics Anonymous. The father had been "talked to" in previous types of couseling sessions. However, after silently viewing K-F-D 129 with his wife and children, he suddenly made a healing decision, not from the world of words but from the silence of his heart. One picture is often worth a thousand words.

DRAWING 129

CHAPTER 10

K-F-D AND OTHER
PROJECTIVE TESTS

The K-F-D is related historically to other projective tests, such as the Make-a-Picture-Story-Tests (MAPS), as discussed in Chapter 3. Traditional analysis of the Thematic Apperception Test (TAT) (74) provides useful guides for K-F-D analysis – for example, plotting the initiator and recipient of various actions. K-F-D relationship to Rorschach variables such as content and determinants is possible. Thus, the Rorschach determinant of m, indicative of tension, i.e., falling or hanging responses, is obviously applicable to K-F-D actions such as falling or hanging (45).

The relationship between K-F-D and handwriting analysis has been described in a series of articles (4, 61). K-F-D 130 and 131 show some features relating the two projective devices.

DRAWING 130

252

K-F-D 130 was drawn by mother 14 months after the family took up residence in Algeria. Note how closely the family is drawn. Note the feet sketched lightly, suggesting a lack of rootedness. The father is large and dominating.

DRAWING 131

K-F-D 130 was drawn by mother 14 months after the family returned to the United States from Algeria. The family is close but separate figures are emerging. The clearly defined feet are suggestive of rootedness. The father is not dominant and is in proportion.

Handwriting analysis, which studies such variables as pressure, stroke or line characteristics, size, placement, connectedness, and styles, has significant similarities and relationships to Human-Figure-Drawing and Kinetic-Family-Drawing analysis, as described in the Appendix.

253

CHAPTER 11

CONCLUSION

The purpose of this book has been to demonstrate and summarize the use of the K-F-D as a scientific tool and as a practical clinical tool in the art of therapy.

The Kinetic Family Drawing Self (K-F-D-S) has been shown to be different from the widely used Draw-A-Person Self (D-A-P-S). The K-F-D-S may be viewed as a *nuclear self* formed early by family dynamics. The D-A-P-S may be viewed as the *environmental self*. At times, particularly in integrated people, these two selves may be the same. However, in the vast majority of people the nuclear self and environmental self are very different.

One more style, Bird's Eye View, has been added to the original seven K-F-D styles discussed in K-F-D II (14). More styles are waiting to be discovered.

The moon as a K-F-D symbol has been added and discussed. The addition of more K-F-D symbols is a rich field for future growth.

The relation of K-F-D to other projective techniques has been touched upon as well as the use of color in K-F-Ds.

The practical use of K-F-Ds in child abuse, family counseling, and evaluation of therapeutic effectiveness research has been discussed. Combining K-F-D computer variables for predictive statistics may be practical, as well as turning artistic K-F-D descriptions into computer statements. For example:

"This K-F-D depicts a cold, segmented, frightening atmosphere with uncaring, non-nurturing, distant parental figures vaguely perceived. The self is incomplete, small, warped or non-relating in a family one would definitely not like to live in,"

may become

"SADDAD + SADMOM + MASSEL + SIZIL + DIRMOM + DIRDAD + COMPART + TENDAD + TENMOM."

"This K-F-D depicts a warm, growth-producing atmosphere including nurturing, friendly parental figures wholly perceived. The self appears whole, growing, relating to and being related to in a family setting one would definitely like to live in,"

may become

"LILIF + NURMOM + NURDAD + COOPDA + COOPMA + FACEXD + FACEXM + BODDAD + BODMOM + BODSEL + SIZSEL."

Such repeatable, easily obtained, and quantifiable K-F-D descriptions could be used in helping to decide:

1) Which foster or adoptive home would be optimal for placement.
2) In a divorce, which parent would provide a more adequate home environment for self-growth.
3) Which culture or subculture provides a family grouping conducive to development of a loving, caring, growing, and peaceful adult.

The school and the culture are extensions of the family. Understanding and improving family conditions for self-growth are a first step in developing a nurturing, peace-loving person.

APPENDIX

Here are some general hypotheses regarding variables used in human figure drawings.

I. PRESSURE FACTORS
    A. Unusually heavy pressure suggests:
        1. Extremely tense individuals (Buck, 10; Hammer, 35; Jolles, 41; Machover, 54)
        2. Organic conditions, possibly encephalitis or an epileptic condition (Buck, 10; Dileo, 26; Hammer, 35; Jolles, 41; Machover, 54)
        3. Assertive, forceful, ambitious persons (Alschuler & Hattwick, 1; Machover, 54)
        4. Aggressive and possibly acting-out tendencies (Petersen, 61)
    B. Unusually light pressure suggests:
        1. Inadequately adjusting individuals (Buck, 10; Hammer, 35; Jolles, 41)
        2. Hesitant, indecisive, timid, fearful, insecure individuals (Jolles, 41; Machover, 54)
        3. Low energy levels (Alschuler & Hattwick, 1)
            Depressive conditions, tendencies toward abulia (Buck, 10; Hammer, 35; Jolles, 41)
II. STROKE OR LINE CHARACTERISTICS
    A. Marked directional preferences:

1. Horizontal movement emphasis suggests weakness, fearfulness, self-protective tendencies, or femininity (Alschuler & Hattwick, 1; Petersen, 61)
2. Vertical movement emphasis suggests masculine assertiveness, determination, and possible hyperactivity (Alschuler & Hattwick, 1; Petersen, 61)
3. Curving line emphasis suggests a healthy personality, possibly suggesting distaste for the conventional (Buck, 10; Jolles, 41)
4. Rigid straight line emphasis suggests rigid or aggressive tendencies (Buck, 10; Jolles, 41)
5. Continuous changes in direction of stroke suggest low security feelings (Petersen, 61; Wolff, 76)

B. Quality of strokes:
1. Firm, unhesitating, determined quality suggests secure, persistent, ambitious persons (Petersen, 61)
2. Vacillating direction, vague lines, and interrupted strokes suggest insecurity, vacillating tendencies (Wolff, 76)
3. Uninterrupted straight strokes have been associated with quick, decisive, assertive persons (Alschuler & Hattwick, 1; Hammer, 35)
4. Interrupted, curvilinear strokes suggest:
   a. Slowness; indecisive persons (Petersen, 61)
   b. Dependent, emotional tendencies (Alchuler & Hattwick, 1; Hammer, 35)
   c. Femininity and submissiveness (Alschuler & Hattwick, 1; Machover, 54)

C. Length of strokes:
1. Long strokes suggest controlled behavior, sometimes to point of inhibition (Alschuler & Hattwick, 1; Hammer, 35)
2. Short discontinuous strokes suggest impulsive excitable tendencies (Alschuler & Hattwick, 1; Hammer, 35)
3. Very short, circular, sketchy strokes suggest anxiety, uncertainty, depression and timidity (Buck, 10; Hammer, 35; Jolles, 41)

D. Shading and shaded strokes suggest anxiety:
1. (Buck, 10; Burns & Kaufman, 14; Hammer, 35; Machover, 54)

III. SIZE OF DRAWING

A. Unusually large drawings suggest:

1. Aggressive tendencies (Buck, 10; Hammer, 35; Machover, 54)
2. Expansive, grandiose tendencies (Machover, 54)
3. Feelings of inadequacy with compensatory defenses (Buck, 10; Hammer, 35; Machover, 54)
4. Possible hyperactive, emotional, manic conditions (DiLeo, 26; Machover, 54)

B. Unusually small drawings suggest:
1. Feelings of inferiority, ineffectiveness or inadequacy (Buck, 10; Burns & Kaufman, 14; Hammer, 35)
2. Withdrawal tendencies in restrained, timid, shy persons (Alschuler & Hattwick, 1; Buck, 10; Hammer, 35)
3. Feelings of insecurity (Alschuler & Hattwick, 1; Buck, 10; Burns & Kaufman, 14)
4. Possible depressive tendencies (Machover, 54)
5. Possible weak ego structure or low ego strength (Hammer, 35; Machover, 54)
6. Regressive tendencies (Machover, 54)
7. When high on page, low energy level, lack of insight, unjustified optimism (Machover, 54)

IV. PLACEMENT OF DRAWINGS
A. Central placement suggests:
1. Normal, resonably secure person: This is most common placement at all ages (Wolff, 76)
2. In absolute center of page, insecurity and rigidity, especially rigidity in interpersonal relations (Buck, 10; Jolles, 41; Machover, 54)

B. Placement high on page suggests:
1. High level of aspiration; striving hard for difficult goals (Buck, 10; Jolles, 41)
2. Optimism, frequently unjustified (Machover, 54)

C. Placement low on page suggests:
1. Feelings of insecurity (Buck, 10; Burns & Kaufman, 14; Jolles, 41)
2. Feelings of inadequacy (Buck, 10; Burns & Kaufman, 14; Hammer, 35; Jolles, 41)
3 Depressive tendencies, perhaps with defeatist attitudes (Buck, 10; Hammer, 35; Jolles, 41; Machover, 54)

D. Placement on edge or bottom of paper suggests:
1. Need for support associated with feelings of insecurity and low self-assurance (Buck, 10; Burns & Kaufman, 14; Hammer, 35; Jolles, 41)

2. Dependency tendencies and a fear of independent action (Hammer, 35)
3. Tendency to avoid new experiences or remain absorbed in fantasy (Jolles, 41)

V.   DRAWINGS OF PERSONS
A. Unusually large heads suggest:
1. Overvaluation of intelligence or high intellectual aspirations (Buck, 10)
2. Dissatisfaction with one's physique (Buck, 10)
3. Possible organicity or preoccupation with headaches (DiLeo, 26)
4. Possible subnormal intelligence (Machover, 54)
5. Children normally draw proportionately larger heads than adults (Machover, 54)
B. Unusually small heads suggest:
1. Feelings of inadequacy or impotency – intellectually, socially or sexually (DiLeo, 26; Jolles, 41; Machover, 54)
2. Feelings of inferiority or weakness (Burns & Kaufman, 14; Machover, 54)

VI.   HAIR TREATED UNUSUALLY
A. Hair emphasis on head, chest, beard or elsewhere suggests:
1. Virility strivings; sexual preoccupation (Buck, 10; Jolles, 41; Machover 54)
2. Probable narcissism with elaborate coiffures, exceptionally wavy and glamorous hair, usually with other cosmetic emphasis; posible psychosomatic or asthmatic condition, or narcissism as in adolescent females, perhaps with inclination toward sexual delinquency (Buck, 10; Machover, 54)
B. Hair omitted or inadequate suggests:
1. Low physical vigor (Machover, 54)

VII.   FACIAL FEATURES TREATED UNUSUALLY
A. Omission of facial features with rest adequately drawn suggests:
1. Evasiveness and superficiality in interpersonal relationships (Burns & Kaufman, 14; Machover 54)
2. Inadequate environmental contact (Machover, 54)
3. Poor prognosis in therapy; satisfactory drawings of features suggests favorable prognosis (Machover, 54)
B. Dim facial features suggest:
1. Withdrawal tendencies, especially when in profile (Machover, 54)

2. Timidity and self-consciousness in interpersonal relations (Burns & Kaufman, 14; Machover, 54)

C. Overemphasis and strong reinforcement of facial features suggest:

1. Feelings of inadequacy and weakness compensated by aggressive and socially dominant behavior (Machover, 54)

VIII. EYES AND EYEBROWS DRAWN UNUSUALLY

A. Unusually large eyes suggest:

1. Suspiciousness, ideas of references, or other paranoid characteristics, perhaps with aggressive acting-out tendencies, especially if eyes are dark, menacing, or piercing (DiLeo, 26; Machover, 54)
2. Possible anxiety, especially if shaded (Machover, 54)
3. Hypersensitivity to social opinion (Machover, 54)
4. Extraversive, socially outgoing tendencies (Machover, 54)
5. Possible voyeuristic tendencies (Machover, 54)
6. Females normally make larger and more detailed eyes than do males (Machover, 54)

B. Unusually small or closed eyes suggest:

1. Introversive tendencies (Machover, 54)
2. Self-absorption; contemplative, introspective tendencies (Machover, 54)
3. Large orbit of eye with tiny eye, strong visual curiosity and guilt feelings, probably regarding voyeuristic conflicts (Machover, 54)
4. Pupils omitted, so-called "Empty Eye," suggests an introversive self-absorbed tendency in persons not interested in perceiving their environment and who perceive it only as vague and undifferentiated (Burns & Kaufman, 14; Machover, 54)

C. Eyebrows and eyelashes treated unusually:

1. Considerable elaboration, especially with very trim eyebrows, may reflect a critical attitude toward uninhibited behavior, with tendencies toward refinement and good grooming, perhaps overgrooming (Machover, 54)
2. Bush eyebrows suggest tendencies away from refinement and good grooming toward "primitive, gruff, and uninhibited" tendencies (Machover, 54)
3. Raised eyebrows suggest an attitude of disdain (Machover, 54)

    4. Eyelashes detailed by males suggest possible homosexual tendencies (Machover, 54)

IX. EARS AND NOSE
  A. Large ears, strongly reinforced or viewed through transparent hair, suggest:
    1. Possible auditory handicap and associated concern (DiLeo, 26; Machover, 54)
    2. Sensitivity to criticism (Buck, 10; Jolles, 41; Machover, 54)
    3. Possible ideas of reference (Burns & Kaufman, 14; Machover, 54)
  B. Nose emphasis through pressure or size suggests:
    1. Sexual difficulties and/or castration fears (Buck, 10; Hammer, 35; Jolles, 41; Machover, 54)
    2. Feelings of sexual inadequacy or impotency, especially in older males, (Machover, 54)
    3. With nostril indicated and emphasized, aggressive tendencies, and indication of association with psychosomatic asthmatic conditions (Burns & Kaufman, 14; Machover, 54)

X. MOUTH AND CHIN
  A. Mouth emphasis suggests:
    1. Regressive defenses, orality (Burns & Kaufman, 14; Jolles, 41; Machover, 54)
    2. Oral emphasis in personality (DeLeo, 26; Machover, 54)
    3. Primitive tendencies (Machover, 54)
    4. Possible speech problems (Machover, 54)
  B. Mouth omitted suggests:
    1. Possible psychosomatic respiratory, asthmatic conditions (Machover, 54)
    2. Possible depressive conditions (Machover, 54)
    3. Reluctance to communicate with others (Buck, 10)
  C. Miscellaneous treatment of mouth:
    1. Teeth showing, in adult drawings, suggests infantile, aggressive or sadistic tendencies (Buck, 10; Burns & Kaufman, 14; Machover, 54)
    2. Short heavy line for mouth suggests strong aggressive impulses but anticipated retaliation makes the individual cautious (Machover, 54)
    3. Single line mouths in profile suggest considerable tension (Machover, 54)
    4. Wide upturned line effecting a grin, normal with children, but in adults suggests forced congeniality, and possibly inappropriate affect (Machover, 54)

5. Cupid bow mouth in female figures has been associated with sexually precocious adolescent females and adult psychosomatic, asthmatic conditions (Machover, 54)
6. Open mouths suggest oral passivity (Machover, 54)
7. Objects in mouth such as cigarettes, toothpicks, pipes, etc. suggest oral erotic needs (Machover, 54)

D. Chin unusually emphasized suggests:
1. Possible aggressive, dominance tendencies (Buck, 10; Jolles, 41, Machover, 54)
2. Possible strong drive levels (Machover, 54)
3. Possible compensation for feelings of weakness (Machover, 54)

XI. NECK AND ADAM'S APPLE TREATED UNUSUALLY

A. General considerations:
1. The neck, connecting link between head and body, has been regarded widely as the symbolic link between intellect and affect. Long necks are associated with dependency in the interpretation of human figure drawings. Most often, interpretive hypotheses regarding the neck are based on this rational (Burns & Kaufman, 14; Machover, 54)

B. Unusually short, thick necks suggest:
1. Tendencies to be gruff, stubborn, "bull-headed" (Machover, 54)
2. Impulse proclivities (Machover, 54)

C. Necks unusually long suggest (see exceptionally long and thin necks):
1. Cultured, socially stiff, even rigid, formal, overly moral persons (Machover, 54)
2. Dependency (Burns & Kaufman, 14)

XII. CONTACT FEATURES (ARMS, HANDS, FINGERS, LEGS, FEET) TREATED UNUSUALLY

A. Arms treated unusually: Generally the condition of the arms and their placement in the drawing reflects the condition and mode of a person's physical or manual contact with his environment.
1. Stiff arms at sides suggest a rigid, compulsive, inhibited personality (see under Stance) (Buck, 10; Jolles, 41; Machover, 54)
2. Limp arms at sides suggest a generally ineffective personality (DiLeo, 26; Machover, 54)
3. Akimbo arms suggest well-developed narcissistic or "bossy" tendencies (Machover, 54)

262

4. Mechanical, horizontal extension of arms at right angles to body suggest a simple, regressed individual with shallow, affectless contact with his environment (Machover, 54)

5. Frail, flimsy, wasted, shrunken arms suggest physical or psychological weakness, feelings of inadequacy (Buck, 10; Hammer, 35; Jolles, 41; Machover, 54)

6. Reinforced arms, especially with emphasis on muscles, suggest power strivings, usually of a physical nature; when associated with broad shoulders, etc., have been linked with aggressive, assaultive tendencies (Burns & Kaufman, 14; Jolles, 41; Machover, 54)

7. Long, strong arms suggest acquisitive and compensatory ambition, need for physical strength, and active contact with the environment (Buck, 10; Jolles, 41; Machover, 54)

8. Very short arms suggest lack of ambition, absence of striving with feelings of inadequacy (Buck, 10; Burns & Kaufman, 14; Jolles, 41)

9. Omission of arms suggests guilt feelings, as with omitted hands, and extreme depression, general ineffectiveness, dissatisfaction with the environment, and strong withdrawal tendencies (Machover, 54)

10. Omission of arms in drawing the opposite sex suggests the person feels rejected by members of the opposite sex, perhaps by subject's opposite-sexed parent; occasionally reflects guilt feelings (Machover, 54)

B. Hands treated unusually:

1. Vague or dim hands suggest a lack of confidence in social situations, or general lack of confidence or productivity, possibly both (Machover, 54)

2. Shaded hands suggest anxiety and guilt feelings, usually associated with aggressive or masturbatory activity (Buck, 10; Jolles, 41; Machover, 54)

3. Unusually large hands suggest aggressiveness (Burns & Kaufman, 14)

4. Hands covering the genital region suggest autoerotic practices, and have been noted in drawings by sexually maladjusted females (Buck, 10; Machover, 54)

5. Swollen hands suggest inhibited impulses (Machover, 54)

6. Omission of the hands is of equivocal significance because they are the most frequently omitted feature of

human drawings. However, this omission has been associated with feelings of inadequacy, castration fears, masturbatory guilt, and organic conditions (Buck, 10; Hammer, 35)

7. Hands drawn last suggest feelings of inadequacy and a reluctance to make contact with the environment (Buck, 10)

8. Fingers obscured by mitten-type hands suggest repressed, suppressed or aggressive tendencies where the aggression may be expressed in more evasive ways, perhaps in furtive outbursts (Buck, 10; Jolles, 41; Machover, 54)

C. Fingers treated unusually: Generally the treatment of the fingers is often considered more important than treatment of the hands or arms; genetically, fingers are drawn before hands or arms. Fingers represent contact features in the strictest sense and obviously may be used in a wide variety of friendly, constructive, hostile, and destructive ways.

1. Talon-like, dark straight lines, or spiked fingers suggest infantile, primitive, aggressive tendencies (Buck, 10; Hammer, 35; Jolles, 41; Machover, 54)

2. Clenched fists suggest aggression and rebelliousness (Buck, 10; Machover, 54)

3. Fingers without hands, common in children's drawings, suggest in adult drawings regression and infantile aggressive, assaultive tendencies, especially if in single dimension with heavy pressure (Machover, 54)

4. Severely shaded or reinforced fingers generally have been regarded as indicative of guilt feelings and usually are associated with stealing or masturbation (Machover, 54)

5. Unusually large fingers suggest aggressive, assaultive tendencies (Burns & Kaufman, 14)

D. Legs treated unusually:

1. Very long legs suggest a strong need for autonomy (Buck, 10; Jolles, 41)

2. Very short legs suggest feelings of immobility and constriction (Buck, 10; Jolles, 41)

3. Refusal to draw legs, usually associated with refusal to draw the figure below the waist, or if only a very few sketchy lines are used, suggests an acute sexual disturbance or pathological constriction (Jolles, 41; Machover, 54)

E. Feet treated unusually:
   1. Elongated feet have been associated with strong security needs and possible castration fears (Buck, 10; Burns & Kaufman, 14; Hammer, 35; Jolles, 41)
   2. Small, especially tiny feet have been associated with insecurity, constriction, dependence, and various psychosomatic conditions (Buck, 10; Jolles, 41; Machover, 54)
   3. Resistance to drawing feet suggests depressed tendencies, discouragement; frequently seen in drawings of physically withdrawn, including bedridden, patients (Machover, 54)
   4. Lack of feet common in runaways (Burns & Kaufman, 14)

XIII. STANCE CHARACTERISTICS
   A. Wide stance suggests:
      1. Aggressive defiance and/or insecurity (Buck, 10; Jolles, 41; Machover, 54)
      2. Especially when figure is in middle of page, aggressiveness, even assaultive aggressiveness, sometimes counteracted by insecurity and manifested by feet which are tiny, shaded, reinforced, or perhaps drawn by light pressure or the consistent use of ground lines (Machover, 54)
      3. When legs float into space and the whole figure slants, severe insecurity and dependency, as in chronic alcoholism (DiLeo, 26; Machover, 54)
      4. When the line fades out with a drawing as described in interpretation 2 above, this may suggest hysteria, psychopathy, or hysterical psychopathy (Machover, 54)

XIV. OTHER PARTS OF BODY (TRUNK, SHOULDERS, BREASTS, WAISTLINE, HIPS, BUTTOCKS, JOINTS, ETC.) TREATED UNUSUALLY
   A. General considerations: Characteristically, the body has been associated with basic drives. The development of drives and activity potentials, growth and decline, and attitudes related to these conditions may be indicated by one's treatment of the trunk. Consequently, treatment of the trunk is more changeable with age. Frequently the trunk is drawn as a relatively simple, more or less rectangular to oval shape. Deviations from this must be considered unusual.
   B. Trunk treated unusually:
      1. Rounded trunks suggest a passive, less aggressive,

265

relatively feminine, or perhaps infantile, regressive personality (Petersen, 61; Machover, 54)

   2. Angular figures suggest a relatively masculine personality (Machover, 54; Petersen, 61)

   3. Disproportionately small trunks suggest a denial of drives, feelings of inferiority, or both (Buck, 10)

   4. Reluctance to close bottom of trunk suggests sexual preoccupation (Machover, 54)

C. Shoulders treated unusually: Generally, the treatment of shoulders is considered an expression of feelings of need for physical power.

   1. Squared shoulders suggest aggressive, hostile tendencies (Buck, 10; Hammer, 35; Jolles, 41)

   2. Tiny shoulders suggest inferiority feelings (Buck, 10; Jolles, 41)

   3. Erasure, reinforcement, or uncertainties in drawing shoulders suggest drive for body development; masculinity is a basic preoccupation; these signs are found in drawings of psychosomatic, hypertense patients (Machover, 54)

   4. In males, massive shoulders suggest aggressive tendencies or sexual ambivalence, often with a compensatory reaction, as in insecure individuals and adolescents (Hammer, 35; Machover, 54)

D. Breasts treated unusually suggest:

   1. Unusually large breasts drawn by males suggest probable strong oral and dependency needs (Machover, 54)

E. Under-clothed or nude figures suggest:

   1. Infantile, sexually maladjusting personalities, as with over-clothing (Machover, 54)

   2. Voyeuristic tendencies (Machover, 54)

   3. Exhibitionistic tendencies (Machover, 54)

F. Clothes too big for figures suggest:

   1. Feelings of inadequacy and self-disdain (Buck, 10; Hammer, 35)

G. Transparent clothing suggests:

   1. Voyeuristic and/or exhibitionistic tendencies (Machover, 54)

H. Button emphasis suggests:

   1. Dependent, infantile, inadequate personality (Burns & Kaufman, 14; Jolles, 41; Machover, 54)

2. Regression, particularly when drawn mechanically down the middle (Buck, 10; Jolles, 41; Machover, 54)

3. On cuffs, adds an obsessive tone to the dependency (Machover, 54)

I. Pocket emphasis suggests:

1. Infantile, dependent male personality (Machover, 54)

2. Affectional or maternal deprivation, which often contributes to psychopathic proclivities (Machover, 54)

3. Large pockets emphasized, adolescent virility strivings with conflict involving emotional dependence on mother (Machover, 54)

J. Tie emphasis suggests:

1. Feelings of sexual inadequacy, especially in adolescents and men over 40 years old (Buck, 10; Jolles, 41; Machover, 54)

2. Tiny, uncertainly drawn, or debilitated ties suggest despairing awareness of weak sexuality (Machover, 54)

3. Long and conspicuous ties suggest sexual aggressiveness perhaps overcompensating for fear of impotence (Machover, 54)

K. Shoe emphasis suggests:

1. Large shoe suggests need for stability (Burns & Kaufman, 14)

2. With over-detailing of shoes, laces, etc., obsessive and distinctly feminine characteristics, most commonly observed in pubescent girls (Machover, 54)

XV. MISCELLANEOUS MODES OF DRAWING EMPHASIZED

A. Stick figures suggest:

1. Evasive tendencies characteristic of the insecure (Buck, 10; Burns & Kaufman, 14; Hammer, 35)

2. Minimal cooperation suggesting negativism (Hammer, 35)

B. Snowman suggests emotional deprivation (Burns & Kaufman, 14)

XVI. MISCELLANEOUS DRAWING CHARACTERISTICS OF PERSONS

A. Transparencies:

1. Showing parts of body through the clothing suggests voyeuristic tendencies in adults, though may be normal in children (Machover, 54)

2. May be associated with organic problems (DiLeo, 26)

B. Excessive erasures suggest:
1. Uncertainty, indecisiveness, and restlessness (Hammer, 35; Machover, 54)
2. Dissatisfaction with self (Hammer, 35)
3. Possible anxiety (Machover, 54)

REFERENCES

1. ALSCHULER, R.H. and HATTWICK, L.W.: *Painting and Personality, A study of Young Children* (Vol. 2) Chicago: University of Chicago Press, 1947.
2. ANASTASI, A. and FOLEY, J.P., Jr.: A survey of the literature on artistic behavior in the abnormal. Ell. Spontaneous productions. *Psychol. Monogr.*, 62:52, 71ff., 1940.
3. ROSENZWEIG, M.R. and PORTER, L.W. (Eds.) *Annual Review of Psychology*, Vol. 27. Palo Alto, CA: Annual Reviews, Inc. 1976, p. 560.
4. ATKINSON, A.T.: John's family in kinetic family drawings. *The Commentary*. 1(3), 1977. Bountiful, UT: Carr Publishing Co.
5. BENDER, L.: Art and therapy in the mental disturbances of children. *J. Nerv. Ment. Dis.*, 86: 249-263, 1937.
6. BOLGAR, H., and FISCHER, L.K.: Personality projection in the world test. *Amer. J. Orthopsychiat.*, 17: 117-128, 1947.
7. BRITAIN, S.D.: Effect of manipulation of children's effect on their family drawings. *Journal of Projective Techniques and Personality Assessment*, 34: 324-327, 1970.
8. BRITAIN, S.D.: The effects of stress and gratification of the family drawings of young children. Unpublished master's thesis, San Jose State College, CA, 1966.
9. BROWN, T.R.: KFD in evaluating foster home care. Olympia, Washington: Office of Research State of Washington, Dept. of Social and Health Services, 1977.
10. BUCK, J.N.: The H-P-T technique: A qualitative and quantitative scoring manual. *J. Clin. Psychol*, 4: 317-396, 1948.
11. BUHLER, C. and KELLEY, G.: *The World Test. A Measurement of Emotional Disturbance*, New York: The Psychological Corporation, 1941.
12. BURNS, R.C. and KAUFMAN, S.H.: *Kinetic Family Drawings (KFD): Psychological Assessments.* London: Abnormal Psychology CRM Books, 1970, p. 384.
13. BURNS, R.C. and KAUFMAN, S.H.: *Kinetic Family Drawings (K-F-D): An Introduction to Understanding Children Through Kinetic Drawings.* New York: Brunner/Mazel, 1970.
14. BURNS, R.C. and KAUFMAN, S.H.: *Actions, Styles and Symbols in Kinetic Family Drawings (K-F-D). An Interpretative Manual.* New York: Brunner/Mazel, 1972.

15. BURNS, R.C.: What children are telling us in their human figure drawings. Early Childhood Educ. Council. Vol. 11, No. 3. Saskatoon, Saskatchewan, Canada, 1980.
16. BURNS, R.C.: Kinetic Family Drawings: Practice and research panel. Annual Meeting of The American Association of Psychiatric Services for Children. November, 1979, Chicago. Taperecording. Audio Transcripts Ltd., New York, N.Y.
17. BURNS, R.C. and KAUFMAN, S.H.: *K-F-D*, Spanish Edition. Editorial Paidos; Defense 599-1 Piso, Buenos Aires, Argentina, 1978.
18. BURNS, R.C. and KAUFMAN, S.H.: *K-F-D*, Japanese Edition. Reimei Shobo Ltd., Ohtsuhashi Building, 3-4-10 Marunouchi, Naka-ku Nagoya-shi Aichi-ken, Japan, 1977.
19. BURNS, R.C. and KAUFMAN, S.H.: *K-F-D*, Great Britain Edition. Constable and Co., 10 Orange St. London WC 2H 7EG, 1977.
20. CASTANEDA, A., McCANDLESS, B.R., and PALERMO, D.S.: The children's form of the manifest anxiety scale. *Child Development*, 27:317-323, 1956.
21. COOPERSMITH, S.: *The Antecedents of Self-Esteem*. San Francisco: Freeman, 1967.
23. CLYDE, D.J.: Multivariate analysis of variance on large computers. Miami, FL.: Clyde Computing Service, 1969.
24. DENNIS, W.: Group Values Through Children's Drawings. New York: John Wiley & Sons, 1966.
25. DESPERT, J.L.: *Emotional Problems in Children*. New York: New York State Hospitals Press, 1938.
26. DiLEO, J.H.: *Children's Drawings as Diagnostic Aids*. New York: Brunner/Mazel, 1973.
27. DIXON, W.J. (Ed.) BMD biomedical computer programs. University of California Publications in Automatic Computation No. 2, Berkeley, CA: University of California Press, 1970.
28. EDWARDS, B.: *Drawing On the Right Side of The Brain*. Los Angeles, CA: J.P. Tarcher, Inc., 1979.
29. FRANK, F.: *The Zen of Seeing*. New York: Vintage Books Random House, 1973.
30. FRANK, F.: *The Awakened Eye*. New York: Vintage Books Random House, 1979.
31. FREEMAN, H.: What a child's drawings can reveal. *Mother*, 35: 34-36, July, 1971, London.
32. FREUD, A. and BURLINGHAM, D. *War and Children*. New York: International Universities Press, 1943, p. 63.
33. GOODENOUGH, F.L.: *Measurement of Intelligence by Drawings*. New York: Harcourt, Brace and World, Inc., 1926.
34. GOODENOUGH, F.L. and HARRIS, D.B.: Studies in the psychology of children's drawing, II: 1928-1949. *Psychological Bulletin*, 47: 396-433, 1950.
35. HAMMER, E.F.: *The Clinical Application of Projective Drawings*. Springfield, IL: Charles C. Thomas, 1958.
36. HARRIS, D.B. *Children's Drawings as Measures of Intellectual Maturity*. New York: Harcourt, Brace and World, Inc., 1963.
37. HEINEMAN, T.: Kinetic Family Drawings of siblings of severely emotionally disturbed children. Thesis Abstracts. School of Social Welfare, University of California at Berkeley, 1975.
38. HULSE, W.C.: The emotionally disturbed child draws his family. *Quart. J. Child Behavior*, 3:152-174, 1951.
39. JACOBSON, D.A.: A study of Kinetic Family Drawings of public school children ages six through nine. Univ. of Cincinnati, 1974. Available through Dissertation Abstracts-Order #73-29-455.

40. JOHNSTON, D.D.: Comparison of DAF and K-F-D in children from intact and divorced homes. Thesis Abstracts. Calif. State Univ., San Jose, 1975.
41. JOLLES, I.: *A Catalogue for the Qualitative Interpretation of the House-Tree-Person (H-I-P)*. Beverly Hills, CA: Western Psychological Services, 1964.
42. KATO, T., IKURA, H., and KUBO, Y.: A study on the "style" in Kinetic Family Drawing. *Japanese Bulletin of Art Therapy*, 7:19-25, 1976.
43. KATO, T. and SHIMIZU, T.: The action of K-F-D and the child's attitude towards family members. *Japanese Bulletin of Art Therapy*, 9:25-31, 1978.
44. KATO, T.: Pictorial expression of family relationships in young children. Ninth International Congress of Psychopathology of Expression. Verona, Italy, 1979.
45. KLOPFER, B., AINSWORTH, M., KLOPFER, W. and HOLT, R. *Developments in the Rorschach Technique*. New York: World Book Co., 1954, p. 114.
46. KOPPITZ, R.M.: *Psychological Evaluation of Children's Human Figure Drawing*. New York: Grune and Stratton, 1968.
47. KUTHE, J.L.: Social schemas. *Journal of Abnormal and Social Psychology*, 31-38, 1962.
48. KUTHE, J.L.: Social schemas and the reconstruction of social object displays from memory. *Journal of Abnormal and Social Psychology*, 64:71-74, 1962.
49. KUTHE, J.L.: The pervasive influence of social schemas. *Journal of Abnormal and Social Psychology*, 68: 248-254, 1964.
50. LANDMARK, M.: Institute of Psychology, University of Oslo, Norway. Personal communication, 1975.
51. LEVENBERG, S.B.: Professional training, psychodiagnostic skill and Kinetic Family Drawings. *Journal of Personality Assessment*, 39: 4, August 1975.
52. LEWIN, K. *Principles of Topological Psychology*. New York: McGraw-Hill, 1936.
53. LOWERY, C.R., ROSS, E., and McGREGOR, P.: The Kinetic Family Drawing. Paper: 31st Annual Meeting of American Association of Psychiatric Services for Children. Chicago, IL, November 1979.
54. MACHOVER, K.: *Personality Projection in the Drawing of the Human Figure*. Springfield, IL: Charles C. Thomas, 1949.
55. McGREGOR, J.: Kinetic Family Drawing test: A validity study. Doctoral dissertation, University of Kentucky, 1978.
56. MacNAUGHTON, E.: Houston, Texas. Personal communication, 1974.
57. McPHEE, J.P. and WEGNER, K.W.: Kinetic Family Drawing styles and emotionally disturbed childhood behavior. Dissertation Abstracts. Boston College, 1975.
58. MILLER, L.C.: School behavior checklist: An inventory of deviant behavior for elementary school children. *Journal of Consulting and Clinical Psychology*, 38: 134-144, 1972.
59. MORENO, F.B.: *Psychodrama*, Vol. 1. New York: Beacon House, 1946.
60. O'BRIEN, R.P. and PATTON, W.F.: Development of an objective scoring method for the Kinetic Family Drawing. *Journal of Personality Assessment*, 58: 156-64, 1974.
61. PETERSEN, C.S.: Roots: As shown in Kinetic Family Drawings. *The Commentary*, 1(3): 1-6, 1977. Bountiful, UT: Carr Publishing Co.
62. RAVEN. J.C.: *Controlled Projection for Children*. London: K.K. Lewis & Co., 1951.
63. REZNIKOFF, M.Z. and REZNIKOFF, H.R.: The family drawing test: A comparative study of children's drawings. *J. Clin. Psychol.*, 12:167-169, 1956.
64. ROTH, J.W. and HUBER, B.L.: Kinetic family drawings. *Familien Dynamik*, 1979, Sonderdruck. Stuttgart: Klett-Cotta.
65. SCHILDKRAUT, M.S., SHENDER, I.R. and SONNENBLICK, M.: *Human Figure Drawings in Adolescence*. New York: Brunner/Mazel, 1972.

271

66. SCHORNSTEIN, H.M.: KFD assessment of how abused children are regarded by their parents. Child Protection Report, Vol. III, No. 1; Washington, DC, 1977.
67. SCHORNSTEIN, H.M. and DERR, J.: The many applications of Kinetic Family Drawings in child abuse. *The International Journal of Child Abuse and Neglect,* June, 1977.
68. SHEARN, C.R., and RUSSELL, K.R.: Use of the family drawing as a technique for studying parent/child interaction. *J. of Proj. Tech. and Person. Assess.,* Vol. 33: 1, 1969.
69. SHNEIDMAN, E.S.: The Make A Picture Story (MAPS) projective personality test: A preliminary report. *J. Consult. Psychol.,* 11:315-325, 1947
70. SIMS, C.A.: Kinetic Family Drawings and the Family Relations Indicator. *Journal of Clin. Psych.,* 30: 87-88, 1974.
71. SOBEL, M. and SOBEL, W.: Discriminating adolescent male delinquents through the use of Kinetic Family Drawings. *Jour. of Personality Assess.,* 40: 91-94, 1976.
72. SOUZA de JOODE, M.: O desenho cinetico da familia (KFD) como instrumento de diagnostico da dinamica do relacionamento familiar. *Auquivos Brasileiros de Psicologia Aplicada,* 29 (2): 149-162, Abr/Jun 1976. Rio de Janeiro, Brazil.
73. THOMPSON, P.L.: Kinetic Family Drawings of adolescents. Dissertation Abstracts. California School of Professional Psychology, San Francisco, California, 1975.
74. TOMKINS, S.S.: *The Thematic Apperception Test: The Theory and Practice of Interpretation.* New York: Grune and Stratton, 1948.
75. WEINSTEIN, L.: Social experience and social schemata. *Journal of Personality and Social Psychology,* 6(4): 429-434, 1967.
76. WOLFF, W.: *The Personality of the Pre-School Child.* New York: Grune and Stratton, 1946.

INDEX

ACTDAD, 69-70

Actions, Styles and Symbols in Kinetic Family Drawings (Burns and Kaufman), vii

ACTMON, 70

ACTSEL, 70

Adoptive home placement, 8, 134, 255

AGE, 70

Aggression, 260, 261, 263, 265
 checklist on, 69
 and competition, 240
 and obsession, 234-35
 and siblings, 70-71
 and symbolization of weapons, 162-64

Alcoholics Anonymous, vi, 84, 250

Alcoholism, vi, 84, 121, 152-53, 250-51

Algeria, 253

Alschuler, R.H., 62, 256, 257, 258, 259n.

American Indian, 130

Ames, Louise Bates, v-vii

Anatasi, A., 62, 269n.

Annual Review of Psychology, 65

Anxiety, 231-33, 260, 263
 association with body, 120
 prediction of, 69

Argentina, vii

Art therapy, vii

Arms in pictures, 262, 263

Arms in drawings:
 absence of, 26-27, 47
 control with, 210-11, 218-19
 scoring criteria for, 80

Asthma, 259, 261, 262

Ball, symbolization of, 240-41

Barrier number, scoring criteria for, 82

BARRMD, 96

BARRSD, 96

BARRSM, 96

Battering parents, 154

Bender, L., 62, 269n.

B = f (P,E) model, 17

BIRDIV, 95, 254

BMD Biomedical Computer Programs, 69

BODDAD, 96, 255

BODMOM, 96, 255

BODSEL, 96, 255

Body language, vii

Bolgar, H., 63, 269n.

Brazil, vii, 65

Breasts in drawings, 266

Brown, T.R., 66, 269n.

Buck, J.N., vii, 18, 63, 256-59, 261-67, 269n.

Buhler, C., 63, 269n.

Burns, R.C., 63, 65, 258-63, 266, 267, 269n.

Buttocks in drawings, 265-67

Canada, vii

Castration fears, 264, 265

"Cell and Self" lectures, 18-19

Child abuse, vi, 223-26
 counseling for, 226-29
 evaluation of, 234-37

Children's Manifest Anxiety Scale (CMAS), 69

Chin in drawings, 261-62
"Cinderella" complex, 116
Circadian rhythm of sleep-wakefulness, 242-43
Cleanliness and identification process, 116
Clothes in drawings, 266-67
Coldness, symbolization of, 174
Communication level, figure scoring criteria for, 76
COMPART, 255
Compartmentalization and identification process, 126, 177-79, 200, 220-22
Competition:
  and aggression, 240
  and introversion, 242
Compulsion, 262
Computers, vi, 69-71, 83-86, 254
COOPDA, 255
Cooperation, figure, scoring criteria for, 76
Coopersmith Self-Esteem Inventory (SEI), 69
COOPMA, 255
Counseling, evaluation of, 234-36
Cross-cultural studies, 64-65
Cultural conflict and separated child, 130-63
Custody, vi

Dehumanization, 152
Dennis, W., 62, 270n.
Dependency:
  on alcoholic father, 250-51
  needs for, 248
  symbols of, 198
Depression, 152, 166-88, 174, 256
Derr, J., 226, 272n.
Despert, J.L., 62, 270n.
DiLeo, J.H., 62, 63, 256, 258-62, 265, 267, 270n.
DIRDAD, 70, 255
DIRMOM, 255
Displacement of female genitalia, 172
DISTMD, 84
DISTSD, 69, 84
DISTSM, 84
Divorce, vi, 8, 66, 121, 128, 130, 206, 210, 214, 255
Doll Play studies, 63
Draw-A-Family (D-A-F), 28-36, 63
Draw-A-Family (D-A-F) Self, 22
Draw-A-Person (D-A-P), 16, 17, 19, 20, 22, 24-30, 32, 34, 36, 38, 42, 45-48, 51, 54, 58, 60-63, 83, 126

Draw-A-Person (D-A-P) Self, 22, 36, 49, 254
Drawing on the Right Side of the Brain, (Edwards), 4
Dreams of missing parent, 160

Ears in drawings, 261
Edging, 89
Ego structure-strength, 258
ENCAPS, 90
Encephalitis, 256
Encopresis, 146, 191, 196, 234
Enuresis, 146
Environmental self:
  D-A-P-S as, 254
  and nuclear self, 17-61
Epileptic condition, 256
Exhibitionistic tendencies, 266
Expansiveness in drawings, 65
Eyebrows in drawings, 260-61
Eyes in drawings, 260-61
  overemphasis of, 49
  scoring criteria for, 80
  shaded, bound-up feeling in, 51

FACED, 96
FACEDA, 4
FACEM, 96
FACEMO, 70
Faces in drawings:
  absence of, 116, 126-29, 140-44, 148, 156, 166-68, 182, 213, 259
  expressive meaning of, 10, 12, 15, 34
  scoring criteria for, 80, 81
FACESE, 70
FACEXD, 255
FACEXM, 255
Family Drawing Test (FDT), 64
Family Relations Indicator, 66
Family therapy, 238-42
FAMSIZ, 69, 70
FEEDAD, 96
FEEMOM, 96
FEESEL, 96
Feet in drawings, 79, 262
  absence of, 116
  expressive meaning of, 6, 10, 15
  size of, scoring criteria for, 79
Felt-Finger Technique, 64
Fetish for shoes, 51
Figure ascendence, scoring criteria for, 76
Fingers in pictures, 262, 264
Fischer, L.K., 63, 269n.
Fisher's transformations, 66
FOLCOM, 91, 223
Foley, J.P., Jr., 62, 269n.

Foster home placement, 8, 134, 226-29, 255
Freeman, H., 64, 270n.

Germany, vii, 65
Goodenough, F.L., 19, 62-63, 270n.
GRADE, 71
Great Britain, vii, 64, 65
Guilt, 114

Hammer, E.F., 63, 256-59, 261, 263-68, 270n.
Hands in pictures, 262, 263-64
Handwriting analysis, vii
Harris, D.B., 63, 270n.
Hattwick, L.W., 62, 256, 257, 258, 269n.
Heads in drawings, 21, 134, 259
Heineman, T., 66, 270n.
Helos, Greek, 174
Hips in drawings, 265-67
Holland, vii
Homosexuality, 158, 261
Hostile-isolationary behavior, 69, 71
House-Tree-Person technique, 18, 19, 21, 22, 26, 28, 63
Huber, B.L., 65, 271n.
Huber, G., vii
Hulse, W.C., 63, 270n.
Human-Figure Drawing, 253
Hysteria, 265
Hypersensitivity, 260

IBM/370 computer, 69
Idealization of missing parent, 160
Identification process, vi, 6, 32, 45, 49, 60, 99-120
  and cleanliness, 116
  and compartmentalization, 126, 177-79, 200, 220-22
  and culture, 130-63
  and divorce, 121
  fantasy in, 160
  and negative self-image, 112-20, 144
  with nonpersons, 162
  in nuclear family, 121-65
  passive identification, 120
  and positive self-image, 100-111
  and rule breaking, 114
  and self-growth problems, 166, 186
  struggle for, 189, 222
  and withdrawal, 120
Impulse control, 225
Intelligence, psychological test of, 63
Internalization of feelings and values, vi
International Journal of Child Abuse, 223, 225

Introversion and competition, 242
Isolation, 204
Italy, vii

Jacobson, D.A., 65, 270n.
Japan, vii, 64, 65
Johnston, D.D., 66, 271n.
Joints, 265-67
Jolles, I., 63, 256, 257, 258, 261-67, 271n.
Juvenile Court, 225-26

Kato, T., vii, 64, 65, 271n.
Kaufman, S.H., 63, 65, 258-62, 263, 266, 267, 269n.
Kelley, G., 63, 269n.
Kinetic Family Drawings (Burns and Kaufman), vii, viii
Kinetic Family Drawing Self (K-F-D-S), 12, 15, 17, 19, 22, 30, 32, 36, 40, 42, 45, 48, 49, 51, 54, 58, 60, 84, 254
Kinetic-Family-Drawing Research Manual, 68-86
  clinical/computer interpretations of, 83-86
  for computerized study, 69-71
  grid for, 96
  judgment of K-F-Ds and styles, 87-95
  procedure for obtaining of K-F-Ds, 68-69
  quantification of K-F-D actions, 71-82
  ways of viewing, 96-98
"Kinetic Family Drawing Test: A Validity Study" (McGregor), 67
Koppitz, R.M., 62, 63, 271n.
Kuthe, J.L., 64, 271n.

Landmark, M., 65, 271n.
Learning-disabled behavior, checklist on, 69
Legs in pictures, 262, 265
Levenberg, S.B., 66, 271n.
Lewin, Kurt, 17, 271n.
LILIF, 82, 255
LINBOT, 92, 134-35
LINTOP, 93
Little World Set, 63
Longitudinal studies of self-development, vi, 189-222
Lowery, C.R., 67, 271n.

Machover, K., 256-65, 265-68, 271n.
MacNaughton, E., 65, 271n.
Make-A-Picture-Story (MAPS) test, 64
Manifest anxiety, prediction of, 69
MANOVA, 69

Masochism, 77, 262
  scoring criteria for, 77
MASSEL, 255
Masturbation, 263, 264
McGregor, J., 67, 271n.
McPhee, J.P., 66, 271n.
Measurement of Intelligence by Drawing
    (Goodenough), 62-63
Mental age, 17
Missing parent idealization of, 160
Moon, symbolization of, 174-85
Mouth in drawings, 261-62
Multiple analysis of variance
    (MANOVA), 66, 69

Narcissism, 77, 259
Neck-Adam's apple in picture, 262
Nigeria, 3
Norms, developmental, 65
Norway, vii, 65
Nose in drawings, 261
NOSIBS, 70
Nuclear self and environmental self,
    17-61
NURDAD, 96, 255
NURMOM, 96, 255
Nurturing, 78

O'Brien, R.P., vii, 4, 66, 69, 70, 71,
    271n.
Obsessive-compulsive defenses, 120,
    174, 228
Orality, 261, 262
ORDM, 82
ORDS, 4, 6, 70, 82
ORTOTM, 70

Paranoia, 10, 49, 156, 260
Parent missing, scoring criteria for, 81
Passive-aggression, 48, 69, 118-19,
    154-55, 234
Patton, W.F., vii, 4, 66, 69, 70, 71,
    271n.
Pearson product-moment correlation, 66
Peers and social concept, 70
Petersen, C.S., 256, 257, 266, 271n.
Phallic (penis) symbol, 172
Picasso, vii
Piotrowsky, vi
Placement of drawings, 258-59
Poland, vii
POWKID, 70
Pressure factors in drawings, 256
Projective techniques, vi, vii, 252-53
Prosocial behavior, checklist on, 69
Psychodrama, 64
Psychopathy, 265

Psychosomatic conditions, 259, 261,
    262

Ra, Egyptian, 174
Raven, J.C., 62, 271n.
Raw Drawing Variables, 73, 74, 75
Regression, 177, 191, 194, 261, 263,
    266, 267
Regression analysis, statistical, 69
Rejection of parent, 142
Reliability, statistical, vi, vii, 65-66, 226
  inter-scorer, 66-67
Reliability Summary Chart, 66
Reznikoff, H.R., 63, 271n.
Reznikoff, M.Z., 63, 271n.
Rorschach test, vi, 252
Roth, J.W., 65, 271n.
Rule breaking and identification process,
    114
Runaway children, 164
Russell, K.R., 63, 272n.

SADDAD, 255
SADDAS, 84
Sadism, 78, 84, 261
Sadism, figure:
  scoring criteria for, 78
SADISTIC DAD, 84
SADMOM, 255
Schildkraut, M.S., 62, 271n.
Schizophrenia, 156
Schneidman, E.S., 64, 272n.
School and self-concept, 70
School Behavior Checklist (SBCL), 69
Schornstein, H.M., 66, 226, 272n.
Self-concept, 4, 6, 70
  in computerized study, 69
  prediction of, 70
  and school, 70
Self-control, 213
Self-development, longitudinal studies
    of, 189-222
Self-esteem, 213
Self-growth, 223-51
Self-image, 17, 19, 99, 100-120, 144
SEX, 71
Sexuality:
  inadequacy-potency problems,
      169-70, 261, 267
  symbolic aspects of, 172
Shearn, C.R., 63, 272n.
Shoulders in drawings, 266
Sims, C.A., 66, 272n.
SIZDAD, 70, 84
Size of drawing, 69, 70, 79, 84, 255,
    257-58
SIZIL, 255

SIZMOM, 84
SIZSEL, 69, 84, 255
SIZSIB, 70
Snow, symbolization of, 174
Snowman, 267
Sobel, M., 66, 272n.
Sobel, W., 66, 272n.
Social concept and peers, 70
Sol, Roman, 174
South Africa, vii
Souza de Joode, M., vii, 64, 272n.
Spain, 65
Stance characteristics, in drawings, 265
Stick figures, 267
Stroke/line characteristics in drawings, 256-57
Styles, scoring criteria for, 82
Suicidal child, 166-88
Sun, symbolization of, 174
Symbolization, 6
  of ball, 240
  of balloon, 104
  of dependency, 198
  of moon, 174, 177, 180
  sexual aspects of, 172
  of snow-coldness, 174
  of sun, 174
  of weapons, 162

Teeth, scoring criteria for, 81

TENDAD, 255
TENMOM, 255
Tension, figure, 78
  scoring criteria for, 78
Thematic Apperception Test (TAT), 64, 252
Thompson, P.L., 65, 272n.
Trunk in drawings, 262-66
Tuning-out parent, 144-45

UNDLIF, 94

Vaginal symbol, 172
Validity, statistical, vi, vii, 66-67
Values, parental, 114
Violence, 126
Voyeuristic tendencies, 260, 266

Waistline in drawings, 265-67
Water, obsession with, 174
Weapons, symbolization of, 162
Weinstein, L., 64, 272n.
Windows in drawings, 123
Wish fulfillment, 126
Withdrawal, 69, 120, 220-22, 263
Wolff, W., 257, 258, 272n.
Workaholic parents, 148-50
World Test, 63, 64

Zen of Seeing, The (Frank), 4, 270n.